PHENOMENAL GENDER

PHENOMENAL GENDER

**What Transgender
Experience Discloses**

Ephraim Das Janssen

Indiana University Press

This book is a publication of

Indiana University Press
Office of Scholarly Publishing
Herman B Wells Library 350
1320 East 10th Street
Bloomington, Indiana 47405 USA

iupress.indiana.edu

∞ The paper used in this publication
meets the minimum requirements of
the American National Standard for
Information Sciences—Permanence
of Paper for Printed Library Materials,
ANSI Z39.48–1992.

Manufactured in the United States of
America

Cataloging information is available from
the Library of Congress.

ISBN 978-0-253-02886-0 (cloth)
ISBN 978-0-253-02892-1 (paperback)
ISBN 978-0-253-02906-5 (ebook)

1 2 3 4 5 22 21 20 19 18 17

For Clark and Sandra Janssen

Contents

Preface

THERE IS SOMETHING of a tradition among phenomenologists to write of tables—of writing tables, mostly.[1] So, as a preface to my examination of the question of gender, I too describe a table. In fact, I tell of two tables. In my room, the writing table is placed near the east wall, facing west so I can turn my gaze past the computer and out over the room and a slice of Chicago that is visible through the windows. This writing table is a cheap one, purchased while I was a student. It is valuable to me as the table on which I wrote my dissertation, for I am a sentimental phenomenologist, prone to value familiarity and scratches over perfection. The computer sits on the table, and the virtue of both is that I rarely have to notice them. They are simply there while I do research, write, and check Facebook. They are the background of my work, the context in which I am free to pay attention to what is actually interesting and engaging. But at the same time, they are a context that shapes how I am in the space governed by the table. I sit upright, on a desk chair, to use the writing table and raise my arms to the right height to use the keyboard. The table, in a literal sense, shapes me.

My writing table is not a girl, and it is not a boy. Since I speak English and use English almost all the time, it is simply an "it." Were I thinking in German, my table would be masculine; were I speaking Spanish, it would be feminine. The pronoun "it" in English indicates that the writing table is an entity to which I owe no ethical debt; I do not need to worry about the writing table's well-being or opinions regarding the World Cup in order to be a good person. Men, women, and people who challenge these categories can use writing tables, although the products we buy are increasingly marketed to specific genders. I doubt that Germans and the Spanish think of their desks as entities that matter in the way that people do, but this is not indicated by the pronouns used to discuss a table in those languages. *Der* and *la* can be used for inanimate objects and for persons; the indication of animate or inanimate Being must be given in other ways. In all languages, though, the way in which tables matter is in how they are of value to people. This writing table matters; it carries my fondness because of its place in the rite of passage that capped the formal leg of my education. Still, it is something I rarely think much about. It is equipment, which is to say it is valuable because it allows me to direct my attention to work, entertainment, or friends: in phenomenological terms explained in chapter 1, it is mainly *zuhanden* (ready-to-hand) and only occasionally *vorhanden* (present-at-hand).

There is another table in the room. If I lean a bit and look around the computer, I see it there. This table is an object of beauty as much as it is an example of how insights can be derived from the phenomenological method. When I was growing up, this table was called the "coffee table," though it has little to do with coffee. It is a circular black lacquer Japanese dining table that my father, who was a sailor, purchased in Okinawa while on leave. On the table top, rendered in paint and inlaid mother-of-pearl, is a landscape depicting a scene across a valley and Mount Fuji in the distance. Throughout the second half of the twentieth century, this table had children and cats climbing on top and underneath it, making it the center of chasing games. My siblings, nephews, niece, and I took its legs off and put them back on, ate our lunch at this table, and raced our cars on it. Wherever we lived, this table was at the center of our living room and very much at the center of our lives. This table, no less than any other, demands a particular physical as well as historical orientation. Properly speaking, one kneels on the floor to sit at this table, something an overweight Westerner like me would find difficult to do for long in middle age. I rarely use it "properly," although it may also be used "improperly."

This table also demands a cultural and linguistic orientation that is not present in most furniture. The scene painted on the table employs perspective to give a sense of depth and distance. As anyone who has taken a drawing or art history course can attest, the use of perspective in painting is accomplished by specific, quite mathematical technique. This technique is also culturally contingent. The rules of perspective employed by the European tradition are different from the rules of perspective employed by an Asian artist painting in her tradition. I am white and was raised on military bases and in the United States, not immersed in other cultures' ways of doing things.[2] Imagine my surprise when, one day at age fourteen, the marks on this table coalesced into a scene for me! For almost a decade and a half, I had dwelled with this table and had not noticed that the marks on it formed a picture. (As a child, looking at Fuji upside down, I had associated the radiating lines with explosions, but only vaguely.) I had not even known that this circular table had an "up" and a "down" orientation. This revelation resulted from looking differently at an object that had always been there in my life. Prior to the moment of revelation, the lacquer table had been a part of the background of my life. The conceptual shift that occurred when I saw the landscape painted on the table is corollary to what happens in phenomenological terms when fallen Dasein engages its world authentically: earth has always been there, but new possibilities are literally *seen*.

The two tables require different orientations of those who use them. They quite literally shape their users into specific stances as much as they are shaped by users' needs. When I purchased my writing table, I sought one that would fulfill certain criteria: I needed to be able to spread my books out and place a computer on the table. But I also was constrained by the available writing tables on the market and within my budget. I could not afford a bespoke table, and so my way of using this table is constrained by market forces. Writing tables are generally built to specifications that suit the average human adult body, so their manufacturers may garner maximum profit from minimum effort. I am shorter than the average *homo sapiens*, and so my way of using my writing table requires adjustment: my chair sits higher and I need to put a footrest underneath to avoid undue fatigue. Since I am a Westerner, unaccustomed to sitting on the floor in the Japanese tradition, I continue to use the dining table as a coffee table, though its main function in my life is still to denote a given space as "home." We are constrained by our world, what is available to us to engage. At the same time, our particular needs and ways of configuring what is available also shape our world, pushing back against what is available to us and reshaping the world as it exists for all of us. The room in which both tables stand is in an apartment on the eighth floor of a nine-story building. The apartments directly above and below are shaped identically to my own, yet each tenant occupies this space in very different ways. Some use furniture to delineate more "rooms," while others leave the floor plan open. Some have taken great care with decorating, while others simply cram in as many storage boxes as they can. For the most part, the different ways the building is used do not alter the basic structure of the building itself, but sometimes this happens, too. This building used to be a hotel, and the need for it to function as an apartment building radically reshaped the structure of its interior, and how it can be dwelled in, long before I came on the scene.

As furniture and living spaces shape physical comportment, so do social constructions shape how possibilities in life are understood. Social constructions include phenomena like gender, money, race, and language. How people live, what is of value, what options are available, and how we sit to do our work or eat our dinner all depend on the social constructions deployed and how they are employed. The sort of economic theory that governs a culture will determine what students choose to major in, what they choose to do with their money, and what their social, as well as economic, status will be as a result of that major. At a very fundamental level, language governs how the world may be engaged—a person whose native tongue is Vietnamese will literally hear more vocal tones than a person whose mother tongue is English. Nobody individually creates these constructions; everybody always already finds themselves involved in them, and in a very real sense they create individuals, in that they shape possibilities for Being. I argue that people shape social constructions right back, in taking what is available and turning it to specific purposes and aims, subtly changing these constructions as they go along. Others come along and do the same. The result is an ever-shifting world where age, race, class, sex, language, economics, and myriad other ingredients of the world intersect and exert power on one another. Social constructions are never isolated; they push and pull on one another in complicated ways, and any discussion of a given point of intersection will necessarily be incomplete. This is not a story of progress toward utopia, just constant exchange of energy or power. Walking through my living room, I exert power on the air, displacing it and sending it elsewhere. My preferred walking patterns exert power on the floors and rugs, wearing them down. And the arrangement of my furniture exerts power right back on me, directing my movements *here*, rather than *there*. In another, only slightly less obvious sense, social constructions exert power on all of us—given the values of our culture, our language, our age, and our socioeconomic position, race, and gender, we will tend toward *this* career rather than *that* one, *this* option for spending our money rather than *that* one. Each of us tends-toward a little differently, too, because each individual occupies a particular place in the world. Each of us brings particular experiences to the table. Each of us acts as a particular and unique intersection of all the various social constructions that come to bear on us.

Just as I was able to live with a table without really seeing it for so long, so do people live with many social constructions and general presuppositions about the world without really seeing them. Most of the time, people spend money without really taking time to ponder how economic systems work, for instance. When spending money on clothing, a shopper typically heads into the men's or women's section of the store, usually without questioning what the goods available in these sections say about what men and women are understood to be. When something disrupts a consumer or a citizen's train of thought, it makes it possible to see the world very differently. The lacquer table is real. It also serves as a metaphor for a much more cataclysmic turn in how I perceived the world: the experience of realizing I am transsexual precipitated a revolution in my thinking that allowed me to see why my life made so little sense. I was using the wrong standards of perspective—I was measuring myself against the cultural standard of "woman" and failing to make any sense that way. Once I started using the cultural standard of "man," everything made so much more sense—using this set of perspective rules allowed me to see what was there all along. Others soon followed suit. Siblings looking at old photos of me years after my transition began have been heard to exclaim, "How did we not know?" The figure in those photos is so clearly a desperately uncomfortable young man in women's clothing that they too have difficulty believing they did not see it for so long. This upheaval in how my place in the world is understood made the issue of gender very conspicuous to me in a way that it is not for most people. My presence in their lives has made the issue of gender conspicuous to others, to those who care about me to some degree or other. (This includes those who hate me—a transphobic stance is still an engagement of the question of gender, even if it is drawn from problematic premises. Hate takes energy and focus; in order to hate, one must care very much indeed.) Simply by being here, by dwelling in the world and being part of others' worlds, the existence of an individual who transgresses gender norms makes gender as such conspicuous to others.

That is a sticky word, "transgress." It expresses so well what is going on when someone does not conform to whatever may be demanded by a social construction: we "step across" those invisible, but very tangible, boundaries that exist in our world. The idea of transgression may also suggest an ethical failing where none exists but is nevertheless entailed in the way the word is understood. This underlying connotation is key to why gender transgression is in such need of study: people who transgress gender norms (and that is everyone at some time or another) may or may not set out to be outlaws and rebels, but we certainly run the risk of being treated like outlaws for our transgressions. For most people, gender norms work just fine, and the discovery that some find them oppressive may be met with a wide variety of responses. Some are annoyed, others become violently opposed to the very idea that gender norms are contingent, and others still react with delight. Transgression shows us that some operation of power is going on. As Michel Foucault writes, "Transgression is an action that involves the limit, that narrow zone of a line where it displays the flash of its passage, but perhaps also its entire trajectory, even its origin; it is likely that transgression has its entire space in the line it crosses."[3] This is to say, the very nature of transgression is that it shows the limits of the structures that delineate the world, and the limits define the transgression *as* transgression. Lines and limitations show themselves only when they have been crossed. Thus, even while transgression violates an established order, it is also busy illuminating the structure of that order. Transgressors, as steppers-across, are the scouts who find those boundaries and show them to everyone else.

This is why the question of gender needs to be asked: not everybody is going to experience a drastic questioning and reorganization of their identity with regard to gender, yet gender exerts power on everybody. It shapes the course lives may take. For this reason, it seems a very good idea to understand how the phenomenon of gender is experienced, what kind of operations it is performing on people, and what kinds of operations people are performing on it. What is going on when a "pink aisle" appears in stores, marketing pink and purple versions of toys especially for girls? Is this cute and playful inclusion or a sinister indication that the feminine is fundamentally Other? What is going on when higher-education tuition costs rise at the same time that the percentage of women who return to school rises? How are possibilities for Being shaped by this, and is there a need to do anything about that? Gender cannot, of course, be understood independently of economics, language, social class, ethnic identity, and other social constructions. It is in the nature of social constructions to intersect and operate in concert. This examination is, of necessity, limited, since it artificially isolates gender as it is experienced from other aspects of experience. At the same time, it aims to suss out a few opportunities for conceptual shifts that may allow a picture of gender to emerge and be understood in a way that also shifts the perspective of its intersection with other loci of power in the lived world.

Notes

1. Sara Ahmed offers an account of this tendency in her book *Queer Phenomenology*, in which she shows how various accounts of tables illustrate differences in phenomenologists' accounts of experience. Sara Ahmed, *Queer Phenomenology: Orientations, Objects, Others* (Durham, NC: Duke University Press, 2006).

2. One of the most prevalent markers of privilege is that it is not seen as privilege—one's own culture is simply seen as the default, as "how things are," which is why institutionalized racism and sexism are so very difficult to combat.

3. Michel Foucault, "A Preface to Transgression," in *Aesthetics, Method, and Epistemology*, ed. James D. Faubion, trans. Donald F. Bouchard and Sherry Simon (New York: New Press, 1994), 73.

Acknowledgments

THERE ARE A GREAT many people without whom this book could not have been created and to whom I am deeply grateful. Of course, I am grateful to Clark and Sandra Janssen. Nancy Lila Lightfoot, Rebecca Logan, Jay Marchand, Dee Mortensen, Paige Rasmussen, Gayle Salamon, Leyla Salamova, Jonelle Seitz, and the Newgen typesetting team were all instrumental in bringing some still-unpolished ideas to completion. John van Buren, John Davenport, Jennifer Gosetti-Ferencei, Judith Green, Lawrence Hatab, Ann Murphy, and David Putney led me through the many layers of education and scholarship that this project required. Some truly remarkable friends have held my hand and served as my cheerleaders during these years of writing: Janet Halpin, Jude Jones, Twila Jones, Andrew Maselli, Max Metrick, Art Redman, Sarah Shapleigh, and Russ Winslow. I thank them all.

PHENOMENAL GENDER

CHAPTER 1

THE QUESTION OF GENDER

THERE ARE MEN, and there are women, the story goes. Men are strong, rational, ordered, active, unitary, and attracted to women. Women are tender, emotional, creative, and passive; their attention is divided; and they are attracted to men. A man and a woman meet, and, after a period of pursuit and more or less feigned reluctance on her part, they marry, have fat babies, and live happily ever after. So the story goes, anyway, and it is not a difficult story to find. It is replayed in almost every book, film, and television program available; it is presupposed in philosophical, legal, ethical, political, and medical systems. It is one of the dominant discourses of Western culture, one of the myths that lend lives meaningfulness. But is it true?

In one sense, this story is not only true but truth. As a dominant discourse, this story is the rule by which truth is measured for how relationships between men and women are supposed to operate; it is the context of the "ought-to-bes" and "in-order-tos" within which all of us always already find ourselves. It is the norm. But in another sense, it is not true at all. If it were, there would be no need to tell the story; it would just be. As the character Cal puts it in Jeffrey Eugenides's *Middlesex,*

I was beginning to understand something about normality. Normality wasn't normal. It couldn't be. If normality were normal, everybody could leave it alone. They could sit back and let normality manifest itself. But people—and especially doctors—had doubts about normality. They weren't sure normality was up to the job. And so they felt inclined to give it a boost.[1]

The story cannot happen unless there are alternatives, other paths that could be taken. And it is in these other paths that things get really interesting.

This book addresses the relationships that exist between individuals (Dasein) and the social body (*das Man*). There is a great deal going on in these relationships. I argue that the ways in which power operates on individuals produce gender and the persistence of transgressive individuals operates, in turn, on institutions of power. This interrelational, mutual interplay of influences is key to understanding what gender is, and this book is an examination of just how such interplay occurs.

The West is heavily invested in the story it tells of gender, so invested that violating gender norms is dangerous business, which makes urgent an examination of just what gender is and what can be expected of it. In some cases, those who do not fulfill conventional expectations regarding gender are decried as threats to the community.[2] In some cases, they are killed. Even children are killed over this.[3] At times, the difficulty arises as a result of ambiguous or atypical biological sex characteristics, which make it difficult to determine an individual's biological sex and gender, and other times there is no physical anomaly present in those who do not conform easily to gender norms. Those physical conditions referred to as "intersex" or "disorders of sex development" raise questions about the patient's "true gender" and how it is to be determined. Debates over the best way to treat such people are impassioned, and the current trend is to delay treatment as long as is feasible without damaging the patient's health. Some of these questions ask whether transgender people commit fraud by living in the gender roles to which they feel themselves drawn, whether it hurts or helps children to be forced to conform to their assigned gender roles, and what may be made of such people in a world in which only two gender options, the masculine and the feminine, are available.

Current research regarding those who do not fit neatly into the expected categories poses a challenge to a cogent understanding of sex and gender and also to the traditional Western understanding of human nature as a combination of the discrete elements of mind and body. It raises questions about identity and thus how related questions of justice and equality may be understood. It is clear that biological facts about bodies create certain expectations regarding the genders that are associated with them, and I argue that it is no less the case that ideas about gender have an effect on how bodies are understood and classified according to scientifically relevant criteria. Most people expect the sciences to be based in brute facts regarding bodies. But at the same time, without the sciences to classify bodies and articulate their findings, the bodies they examine would not be intelligible; there would be no way of speaking about them at all. Culture, which includes the sciences, has its basis in the natural world. At the same time, nature has its basis in culture, because it is only by means of language and inquiry, which are cultural phenomena, that anything about nature can be known. The philosophical question of gender is concerned with how a loosely related set of expectations that seems to begin with biology but also extends to behavior, social roles, legal status of citizens, the character of freedom, and ultimately human experience itself may be made sense of. The question of gender arises out of the way gender is meaningful in factical, historical life; how gender expectations come about; the role of transgression in the gendering of human lives; and relationships between individuals and the social constructions that shape us. As Martin Heidegger has noted, nonscientific experience and understanding of the world are epistemically and experientially prior to scientific investigations; that is, people do science about things that already matter, instead of things mattering because people do science about them.[4] Thus, the *biological* aspect of gender is not the only important one in the field of gender theory or, indeed, in life; equally crucial are the *existential*, *cultural*, and *historical* origins of gender.

This is why Heidegger's phenomenological model of Dasein (human existence, Being-there) in his most well-known work, *Being and Time*, is useful for articulating the question of gender. Heidegger was innovative; he was the first in twentieth-century Continental philosophy to point out that a defining characteristic of human experience is the very fact that human beings question their own existence. Dasein cares about its own existence while making as few assumptions as possible about what "human nature" is. Employing Dasein allows a perspectival, historical, and deconstructive approach to the question of gender, dismantling the tradition in order to see how it works.[5] Dasein is Heidegger's response to the mess that the Moderns have made of trying to define the self as a discrete, coherent "thing" while never discovering just what that thing is, a minimalist approach that allows for the discussion of ideas that are otherwise precluded by the very language of the philosophical tradition. The stories Dasein tells and the ways in which Dasein investigates its world are what is important and interesting to the phenomenologist, because these are what shape Dasein's manner of living out its own Being in its everyday concerns. Since Dasein is a question to itself, instead of a disembodied, coherent subject or *res cogitans*, it makes sense to speak of many aspects of Dasein's Being, including its body, its culture, and the natural world, as crucial to Dasein's questioning of its own Being. This means that "the 'essence' of Dasein lies in its existence,"[6] which is to say, the question of the meaningfulness of Dasein's embodied Being-in-the-world is not an ahistorical, universal, "essential" answer but rather a mutable, undefined, and unrestricted question that has different historical answers. The point is for Dasein to question its existence as it is lived rather than to produce answers that are reified as "absolute truth."

Heidegger's account of Dasein is a challenge to traditional essentialist metaphysics, and he deliberately avoids describing human beings in essentialist ways that are so familiar as to go un-remarked-on.[7] Instead, Heidegger's project is to "destroy" the basic tenets of the Western philosophical tradition in order to gain a fresh perspective on how they operate.[8] It is not only the thinking of the ancients that must be destroyed in the literal sense of being unbuilt or dismantled but also the philosophical heritage they have passed on. To discover the most basic truths about human Being, it will be necessary first to cast off the lenses of tradition. The idea is not to "destroy" the past in the sense of annulling it *in toto*; rather, it is to discover how much thinking along traditional lines has left hidden.

A most interesting aspect of practical application of ontology is that it provides the means for reversing the usual focus on gender as such and approaching the question from a different angle. The work being done in this field focuses on questions of ethics in particular cases or specific types of cases, rather than on the experience of gender and the ways in which gender is innovated according to those persons' needs.[9] But gender matters only insofar as it is meaningful to Dasein's life, so a reversal of this focus is also necessary to produce a robust account of how gender is experienced and why it is so important. The point is to approach the issue of gender from the point of view of how Dasein lives it, avoiding the danger of endorsing existing gender norms in the process of examining gender norms and thus creating circularity. Instead of asking, "What causes some people to be transgender?" the phenomenologist needs to ask, "What is gender?" To begin, presuppositions regarding gender and how they function in Dasein's lived experience must be examined.

I argue that it is not the case that Heidegger was a hopelessly sexist thinker who must be drastically altered; rather, it is the case that he did not address all the possible implications of his own ontology of Dasein. Insofar as Dasein is a bare-bones model of the kind of being to whom its Being matters and is a question for it, it provides a model with implications that can be developed and applied to gender issues that are in urgent need of attention today. It is my hope that a Heideggerian, applied phenomenological account of gender focuses attention where it is needed: lived experience. I do not want to give a merely sensational report of people who are so bold as to transgress gender norms and expectations; nor do I want to offer an in-depth exegesis of Heidegger; rather, I aim to use Heidegger's theories to get at the heart of what gender is for *all* by examining those for whom gender just does not work out according to expectations. Just as the study of a foreign language aids in understanding one's native tongue, an examination of transgressively gendering individuals can yield a greater understanding of how this ubiquitous phenomenon operates for everyone.

So what is gender? I argue here that it is a phenomenon experienced as a style of Being, shaped by the tensions that obtain between individuating Dasein, understandings of embodiment, and the social constructs according to which Dasein's Being is rendered intelligible, and operating according to deployments of power by means of technologies. Since Dasein is always already engaged meaningfully with its world, this meaningful engagement always takes some historical form, some "style" or other. There is no aspect of Dasein's Being in which gender is not an issue for it. Yet this issue *as* an issue has until recently gone largely unexamined and unquestioned in the history of Western thought, including in Heidegger's own work. Gender differences have been presupposed rather than questioned. Emancipatory discourses concerned with prescriptive ethical or political claims, such as the fights to pass the Equal Rights Act or Employment Non-Discrimination Act, fail to question what gender is, instead adopting prevailing presuppositions regarding gender. If gender is simply not presupposed to be an ahistorical metaphysical or biological reality but rather understood to be a fluid, changing, historical concept that is subject to change, it is possible to examine how it arises and explore where its limitations lie. This can free inquiry from both unfounded biological reductionism and metaphysical essentialism.

To do this, I use Heidegger's model of Dasein but also the theories of Judith Butler, Michel Foucault, Maurice Merleau-Ponty, and Edmund Husserl. The result is an applied ontology of the phenomenon of gender that is neither a critique of current secondary literature in Heidegger studies nor a prescriptive ethics. Rather, this work is an exploration of how it is that Dasein both shapes and is shaped by gender expectations within its particular, specific, historical, and cultural context. My aim is not to place these thinkers into conflict, declaring one the "winner" and the others "losers" in a debate. While agonistic methodologies are quite helpful in establishing validity in competing arguments, this investigation calls for a different approach, one more akin to the way music is read on multiple staves so that harmonies may emerge. It is more helpful to engage in a phenomenological examination of the theories and analyses of the above-named thinkers, which also allows the analyses themselves to cooperate and interrelate in a living understanding of gender.

Wobbly Terms

One difficulty that arises in gender studies is the ambiguity of the terms used. Indeed, this ambiguity demonstrates the urgency and necessity of the present inquiry—discrete terms like "biological sex," "sexual orientation," "sexual behavior," and "gender" are often conflated in everyday, professional, and academic discourse; they are "wobbly." If one asks an expectant mother the gender of her baby, she is likely to say, "It's a boy" or "It's a girl," when in fact, while the fetus's biological sex is known, the child has yet to manifest any gender, properly speaking. Certain expectations are implied in language, not least of which is the expectation that a fetus that has a penis will be a "boy," whereas a fetus that has a vagina will be a "girl." This is most often the case, but, as many parents have discovered, it is not a universal truth. It is necessary, then, in any discussion of gender, to clarify the terms of the discussion in order to avoid confusion and talking past each other. In this book, I rely on the current common, professional, and academic usages of the terms in question, but I recognize, too, that allowing terms to remain a bit "wobbly" in usage may not be such a terrible thing: in different contexts, different ideas (and sometimes even new ones) can emerge. At any rate, care with language should not extend to rigidity that prevents the expression and evolution of ideas.

That said, "biological sex" is used here to refer to the biological classification of bodies as male, female, or intersex (those bodies that are not unambiguously male or female), which takes genital shape, chromosomes, hormones, reproductive capacity, and DNA into account. The evolution of the way in which biological sex of human beings is classified has occurred in conjunction with the discovery of sexual differences between males and females. Primary sex characteristics are those that are related to the reproductive system, whereas secondary sex characteristics are those nonreproductive characteristics that typify males and females.[10] So the presence of testicles or a uterus in a human body is a primary sex characteristic, and facial hair or larger breasts are secondary sex characteristics. Typically, humans are classified as being one of two sexes, but the incidence of bodies being born that do not neatly fit one category or the other is not as uncommon as is ordinarily supposed, and estimates suggest that as many as one in one hundred births exhibit some sort of intersex condition.[11] Such conditions include those in which the genitalia develop in an atypical fashion, in which DNA is atypically structured, in which an insensitivity to, or overproduction of, hormones may occur, or in which enzymes that inhibit masculinization are produced. Since the mid-twentieth century, such conditions in newborns or small children have been regarded as "medical emergencies"[12] and are medically "corrected" as far as possible, whether they threaten the patient's overall health or not. There is today some debate about whether this is the most ethical approach to the phenomenon of intersex individuals, and some very strong arguments are being made in favor of delaying surgeries or hormone treatments (in the absence of medical necessity) until patients are capable of making informed decisions regarding their own bodies.[13]

"Sexual orientation" is a term that refers to an individual's sexual or romantic desire and the object of such desire. Homosexuality, heterosexuality, bisexuality, and asexuality are all characterized by the sex or gender of the object(s) of an individual's desire, if any, and it is the sex or gender of the person desired that identifies the one who desires as having one of these orientations. Sometimes the terms "androphile" and "gynophile" are used instead, so as to indicate an individual's attraction to male or masculine partners, or female or feminine partners, respectively. These terms seat an individual's identity in the object(s) of the individual's desire. Homosexuality, in particular, is frequently conflated with gender transgression. Gay people are sometimes regarded as transgressing gender expectations by virtue of their desire for same-sex or same-gender partners, whether they display any other indications of gender transgression or not, and it is also not uncommon for other gender-transgressive identities, desires, and behaviors to be mistaken for indicators of homosexuality. Indeed, the early psychiatric community believed homosexuality (along with transvestism, intersex conditions, and fetishism) to be mere gender inversion.[14] While it is not the case that all homosexuals transgress gender boundaries, the continued conflation of homosexuality with gender transgression is probably due to the increased visibility of those homosexuals who do transgress gender norms and expectations and the concomitant "closeting" of those who do not. It is now known that sexual orientation is not always manifested in nonsexual gendered behavior discernible to the general public, but these stereotypes nevertheless persist in Western culture. For instance, in the past, transvestism has been taken to be an indicator of homosexuality, but in fact, transvestic fetishism is a diagnosis that specifies that the patient is a heterosexual male.[15] (To be understood as a disorder, transvestism must also cause the patient distress. If there is no distress, transvestism is no longer considered pathological. Thus, uncloseted homosexual drag kings and drag queens do not suffer from transvestic fetishism.)

"Sexuality," which is frequently conflated with sexual orientation, is a component of individual identity and consists of a fluid matrix in which biological sex, gender, and sexual orientation are all at work according to cultural scripts and discourses that render them intelligible and meaningful. Whereas sexual orientation defines an individual as homosexual, heterosexual, bisexual, or asexual in reference to the object of his or her desire, an individual's sexuality refers to the desires themselves, as it intersects with his or her biological sex, gender identity, and capacity for or inclinations toward particular sexual behaviors. Sexuality entails the ways in which the various aspects of biological sex, gender, desire, partners, and actions are interconnected in a given individual's life. Examples of sexuality are an individual's desire to be a dominant partner and preferences for or fantasies of particular acts or relationships with sexual or romantic partners.

"Sexual behavior" refers to the way in which individuals engage in sexual acts. These can be acts of procreation or acts of pleasure, and the category of "sexual acts" is much broader than those that refer to genital stimulation or reproduction. Sexual behavior is not a reliable indicator of the sexual orientation or the sexuality of the agent, as is demonstrated by the prevalence of sexual activity among heterosexuals in single-sex environments, such as prisons; it is also not uncommon for homosexuals to marry members of another sex and have sexual relations with their spouses in spite of their own orientations. Obviously, sexual behavior refers to a broader classification of sexual activity than mere choice of partner. It has to do with the kinds of sex acts in which an individual engages and includes such distinctions as degrees of activity or passivity, sexual positions, paraphilias, fetishes, BDSM, number of partners, swinging, kink, or vanilla. Sexual behavior, then, is concerned with *what* an individual does or desires to do, whereas sexual orientation is concerned with *whom* an individual wants to do it with. Sexual behaviors are also distinct from sexual orientations in that there is choice involved. Human beings do not choose their desires but do choose whether and how to act on desires. So an androphilic individual may choose to engage in only gynophilic behavior, but this does not change the individual's sexual orientation and certainly does not "cure" homosexuality.

"Gender" is a difficult term with many different connotations. Its root is the Greek *genos*, which refers to a family, class, sort, kind, or breed. As it is most commonly used in English today, "gender" refers to the classification of human beings into two types, "men" and "women," with males being supposed to be more or less "masculine" and females supposed to be more or less "feminine"; however, there is nothing inherent in the term "gender" to prevent its being used to classify human beings according to other criteria. In fact, its original meaning was not necessarily so narrow. A broader usage can be found in the German *Geschlecht*, which corresponds to the Greek root of the English term. *Geschlecht* can refer to social expectations that surround biological sex but also to class, race, socioeconomic position, skin color, or even body weight and attractiveness. Any aspect of Dasein's specific Being that is drawn from the shape it takes with relation to others (*Mitsein*) and has to do with the way Dasein's Being is played out in the social sphere might be seen as an enactment of *Geschlecht*, or type. The question of gender as the term is commonly used is every bit as urgent to Being as questions of class struggle, race, or social justice. I find the broadest usage of the term "gender," where it refers to many aspects of social identity, to be helpful at times and to distinguish it from the narrower idea of gender as the social constructions and expectations that are supervened on biological sex, but which are not themselves biological and may be transgressed. When I am using "gender" in this broad sense, I indicate the usage by supplying the German term in parentheses.

An individual's gender identity may or may not conform to social constructions and expectations, and those who do not conform are characterized in this project as "gender transgressive." This is a broad category with deliberately blurry boundaries. I refer to those who cannot, will not, or do not meet the expectations placed on them in the social sphere, for whatever reason, as "gender transgressive." This will no doubt raise some eyebrows, but I maintain that the phrase is appropriate to this investigation. What is being transgressed is social expectation—gender boundaries are literally stepped across by some individuals. Furthermore, this stepping across is often taken as an affront by other community members and institutions. The connotation of "trespass" or "violation of limits" in the definition of "transgression" is important to what gender is and the response experienced by nonconformists. A less well-known connotation of the term refers to the spread of the sea over the land; the sea's transgression accounts for many features of the planet's surface. Gender transgression operates in this way, too, shaping features of experience much as the sea shapes continents. Cultural investment in gender norms and boundaries makes them seem at times to carry the weight of law, and challenges to this investment are taken very seriously indeed. Some choose their transgression, as in the case of the "house husband" and father of a nuclear family who has the luxury of choosing to remain at home to raise the children. Others do not choose at all, as in the case of transgender individuals whose gender identity is different from what is expected. The gender transgressive include, but are not limited to, cisgender[16] individuals who violate norms to achieve some purpose, such as the woman who chooses to work in construction; transgender individuals, who find the gender assigned to them on the basis of biological sex to be an incorrect or incomplete expression of their experience; transsexual persons, who change or desire to change the physical sex characteristics of their bodies by means of hormones and surgeries; transvestites and cross-dressers, who identify themselves as their assigned gender and accept binary gender distinctions but dress in the clothing of the opposite gender for various reasons; homosexuals; lesbians; genderqueer individuals, who reject binary gender distinctions altogether; androgynous individuals; drag performers; and pretty much anyone else who identifies or is identified by others as "queer." I do not endorse gender normativity and use the term "transgressive" as a description of the experience of those who do not conform to gender norms, never as a prescription for behavior. We are criminalized and pathologized. Sometimes, what *is* is not what *ought to be*, and that is why this investigation is needed.

The last two terms I would like to focus on are "social construction" and "norm." These terms are sometimes conflated, but the distinction between them is significant to this project. A social construction is a model or apparatus according to which phenomena and experiences are organized to render them intelligible. In other words, social constructions are conceptual contexts within which experience is understood. In the case of gender and sex, Judith Butler defines a social construction as "the cultural inscription of meaning"[17] on physical bodies and the subsequent understanding of those bodies as being sexed. The model of gender as having two possibilities, masculine and feminine, is a social construction. Some cultures have other possibilities, so their contexts are different.[18] Norms, on the other hand, are descriptions of specific behaviors or aspects of things that are believed to be typical. Social norms arise out of the expectation that individuals will not vary too greatly from what is regarded as standard for their particular demographics or their biological type. How and how much an individual varies from the norm are individuating aspects of that individual's life. Medical records indicate degrees of adherence to or deviation from the norms associated with healthy bodies. In educational systems, students are evaluated according to what the norm indicates that most students of a given age and background can reasonably learn. Norms function as touchstones of what is typical within a given social construction.[19] A striking example of this is the means by which some intersex infants are identified. One possible indicator of an intersex condition is atypical genitalia. If a genital organ presents as outside the norm for what is defined as a penis or for what is defined as a clitoris, the individual is classified as intersex. But the classification "intersex," like "male" and "female," is only meaningful within a social construction that identifies human bodies according to these named types to begin with. So a social construction is the context in which norms arise, and individuals are "typed" within the social construction according to how much or how little they conform to norms.

The use of this terminology varies even within the field of gender studies. This is a young field, and the ways distinctions are drawn are still being hashed out. To clarify how I am using terms, it is helpful to examine a case that exemplifies both the ethical issues surrounding the question of gender and the difficulties that can arise when gender transgression is articulated. Thomas Beatie is a transgender man who gave birth to a child in 2008. During his pregnancy, Beatie wrote about his experience as a pregnant man in the United States in the twenty-first century and published his article in the *Advocate*, a popular magazine that serves the lesbian, gay, bisexual, and transgender (LGBT) community.[20] Beatie and his wife wanted to have children together, but his wife was unable to conceive. Beatie had not had his reproductive organs surgically removed and had the capacity to stop taking testosterone and conceive a child. When the couple decided that Beatie would bear their child, they had a great deal of difficulty finding physicians who would treat them, endured the mockery of clinical staff, and underwent psychological evaluations not normally required of would-be parents to determine their fitness to raise a child. One physician even directed Beatie to shave his facial hair. Beatie decided to write an article relating his story in order to raise public awareness of the issues surrounding gender transgression, particularly the quality and availability of medical care and the legal status of transgender persons. Beatie has suffered disapprobation for making his story public, from both the general population and the transgender community. Many in the general public have expressed dismay or outright rejection of the notion that a man can bear a child, even to the extent of sending death threats to Beatie and his family.[21] At the same time, many in the transgender community feared that the sensationalism of Beatie's visibility caused attention to shift away from social and legal accommodations afforded to transgender persons.[22] As of this writing, Beatie has successfully delivered three children.[23]

When Thomas Beatie was born, his biological sex was female, but since that time, he has undergone surgeries and hormone therapy to alter his secondary sex characteristics and genitalia.[24] His gender is masculine, and he regards himself as being a man within the expectations of the society in which he lives. His social role is that of a man, and the law regarded Beatie as legally male and legally married to a woman in a state that did not then recognize same-sex marriage.[25] His sexual orientation is something I hesitate to speak to, as only Beatie can make any claims regarding this. However, as he has described himself as "deeply in love" with his wife,[26] his marriage could be tentatively characterized as a heterosexual relationship. So Beatie's biological sex after his surgeries and hormone treatments is ambiguous, particularly since he opted to retain his reproductive organs when he underwent sex reassignment surgeries. Beatie is not intersex but rather transgender, which means that he has crossed the boundaries of the sex-gender correlation that is expected by society, and transsexual, since he has altered his body. The difference lies in the fact that the ambiguity of his biological sex is the result of surgeries and hormone treatments and is not a congenital physical condition. Thomas Beatie's sexuality, then, may be indicated by his self-identification as a transgender, heterosexual man. In undergoing sex reassignment surgery and marrying a woman, Beatie has brought his body into greater conformity with his gender identity with regard to the norms and social constructions of the society in which he lives. In having borne children, Beatie transgressed these same norms and social constructions in another way. On the one hand, Beatie is gender transgressive simply by virtue of *being* transgender, because his gender and his body are not in conformity with the expectations of society without the aid of medical intervention. On the other hand, he is gender transgressive in that he is a man who became pregnant, which is nearly culturally unintelligible in a society that regards motherhood as being exclusively an aspect of womanhood. Moreover, when Beatie gave birth, the legal definition of fatherhood in the United States did not apply to the parent who bears the child, but Beatie does regard himself as his children's father, which had the potential to raise issues with his family's legal standing, regardless of the fact that Beatie, his wife, and their children are all United States citizens.[27] The situation in which Thomas Beatie finds himself is one that highlights the difficulties entailed in the predominant conception of gender as intrinsic to biological sex, the acceptance and visibility of persons who transgress gender norms in both the general public and the medical field, and the legal status of those who do not fit into available legal categories.

Gender Studies: A Short, Selective History

The genesis of gender studies is difficult to pinpoint, as it arose out of the distinct yet related disciplines of women's studies, sociology of gender, feminist theory, and queer theory.[28] The focus of gender studies is the lived experience of gender within social groups, although it does refer to biological bases for biological sex, sexuality, and gender. The discipline is also closely associated with race, ethnicity, and class studies. In a broad sense, gender studies is an interdisciplinary field that addresses such issues as the features and characteristics of gender; the masculine-feminine binary; the assumption of heterosexuality; the relationships between gender and identity, the body, culture, epistemology, biology, and politics; the power structures that perpetuate—and challenge—gender roles; social expectations regarding gender; sexual orientation; and the historical performance and conception of gender as the mechanism both by which masculinity and femininity are produced and by which it may be deconstructed.[29]

Gender studies addresses the experiences of women and men, as well as those who self-identify, or are identified by others, as both or neither. Concern with gender identities that do not conform to social expectations is an important development, since, as Luce Irigaray notes, "female sexuality has always been conceptualized on the basis of masculine parameters."[30] This is the paradigm that gender studies challenges. Examining women's issues within a context that only contrasts them with traditional conceptions of the masculine means adopting all the presuppositions that have caused women and the feminine to be devalued philosophically. But examining the phenomenon of gender in and of itself opens the field of study at a point at which not only women's issues but also the issues that affect everyone can be addressed. The upshot of this is that gender theorists are finding that gender itself is a great deal more complex than had previously been supposed. Essentialist theories that assume gender is tied to some essential quality (usually biological) of people have been seriously challenged. The implications of gender studies for various fields of study, including medicine and law, are enormous. The treatment that patients and citizens are to receive at the hands of authorities is at stake.[31] One of the most important tools gender theory has at its disposal is the set of narratives that are produced by those for whom traditional conceptions of gender do not suffice to explain and do justice to their experience. In this sense, gender studies follows in the footsteps of the black civil rights, women's, and gay rights movements in its methodology of gathering narratives that challenge the conventional wisdom of the status quo. These narratives include personal stories, medical treatises, psychological case studies, legal statutes, and interdisciplinary academic theory. They are the stories people tell of gender. They are how people make sense of this phenomenon that affects almost every aspect of life.

Some theorists, such as Simone de Beauvoir and Butler, have noted that the ordinary conception of gender is consonant with theories of biological essentialism. It is true that most people ordinarily do associate biological sex with gender. Biological essentialist feminists take the kind of body designated as female to be the seat of women's experiences and as a kind of unifying element shared by all women. The problem with this is that the understanding of bodies is constructed according to gendered standards of thinking. Not only are there in fact bodies that do not conform to the biological standard of "female" or "male," but the way the sciences classify typical bodies is based in gendered assumptions and concerns. Furthermore, the model of biological essentialism fails to account for differences in the feminine and the masculine across different cultures or eras. If there were a biological basis for gender, these differences could not occur. Biological essentialism is contradictory: it necessitates that gender be both immutable as a biological necessity and mutable, since there are in fact bodies that do not fit neatly into the medical definitions of "male" and "female," and such persons would, by definition, be either both masculine and feminine or neither masculine nor feminine.

Another essentialist line of reasoning regards traditional symbolic conceptions of "the feminine," rather than biology, as the unifying element shared by all women.[32] The problem with this approach is that since it uses traditional characterizations of the feminine to ground claims that (contrary to Western philosophical history) the feminine is to be valued, it fails to account for the fact that these characterizations have defined the feminine precisely as that which lacks value and thus reaches the logical impasse of reinscribing the very way of thinking it seeks to oppose. Accepting the traditional conceptual framework that devalues the feminine as the very framework on which to build the means of valuing the feminine renders this essentialist interpretation of the feminine absurd. If the masculine is, as Western tradition would have it, the rational, the symbolic, and the natural, then there are no terms left with which a discussion of the feminine can be intelligently pursued, since it is characterized from the start as the irrational, the Other to reason, and the anomalous. The problem is that since the very language utilized in undertaking such an inquiry is laden with linguistic presuppositions that favor the masculine, it has already accepted the supposed inferiority of the feminine in setting out to prove the value of the feminine. The logic simply does not follow.

Fortunately, the tradition is contingent. The notion that women can be defined as female-bodied humans and men as male-bodied humans has been under fire since at least 1949, when Beauvoir published *The Second Sex*, with the famous declaration that "one is not born, but rather becomes, a woman."[33] The suggestion is that while one may be born female, it takes many years of rigorous training to make a woman of a female child. "Woman" is a term that refers not only to an adult human with certain biological sexual characteristics but also to a type of person who is expected to fill a particular role in society, to reproduce more humans, to serve as the Other against which man is contrasted and can come to a better understanding of himself. Beauvoir asks, "What place has humanity made for this portion of itself which, while included within it, is defined as the Other? What rights have been conceded to it? How have men defined it?"[34] The answers she finds in nature, in literature, in the sciences, and in social hierarchies reveal a contingency to sex differences that demands to be addressed:

> If the little girl were brought up from the first with the same demands and rewards, the same severity and the same freedom, as her brothers, taking part in the same studies, the same games, promised the same future, surrounded with women and men who seemed to her undoubted equals, . . . [she] would not seek sterile compensation in narcissism and dreaming, she would not take her fate for granted; she would be interested in what she was *doing*, she would throw herself without reserve into undertakings.[35]

In short, women and men are not identical to the biological categories of male and female, and the roles that women and men are called on to perform in society are not as firmly rooted in immutable biological necessity as most suppose. Rather, society is constructed to cultivate the aspects of a female-bodied human being's character that are deemed "feminine." This process, and not biology, typically (but not in every case) produces a feminine person, a productive and reproductive member of society who fulfills a certain kind of role: in short, a woman.

In 1976, Michel Foucault took up this thread of inquiry with the publication of the first volume of his *History of Sexuality*. While Foucault does not reference Beauvoir directly, it is clear that his line of thinking plays very nicely with hers. Whereas Beauvoir dedicates a great deal of attention to an existential-phenomenological account of how a female-bodied child becomes first a girl and then a woman in Western society, Foucault addresses the mechanics of how the power structures that act on all members of modern society regarding sex and gender roles have the effect of producing sexuality as personal identity. Medicine, law, education, and religion all produce discourses that, while seeming to repress sexuality, in fact produce it. These discourses do not tell us *what* to think about sex, sex differences, or gender roles; they tell us *how* to think about these issues. They dictate which aspects of human sexuality are given voice and what is left in silence. By virtue of their methods, then, discourses create sexuality and gender. The Other in Foucault's account is not woman but the perverse. "Normal" sexuality, that which is promoted by medical, legal, educational, and religious institutions, is defined in contrast to pathology. But the more medical and legal discourses study sex and sexuality, the more they generate pathologies. Foucault writes, "Between the state and the individual, sex became an issue, and a public issue no less; a whole web of discourses, special knowledges, analyses, and injunctions settled upon it."[36] This entailed an increasing process of normalization. Certain kinds of sex, or motivations for sex, were regarded as objectively good, normal, and natural. Because reproduction was certainly regarded as beneficial for the church and state, whether sexual acts could result in reproduction became the standard of their moral value. The family structure was regarded as beneficial to society as well, so heterosexual sex within marriage became the standard of value. Medicine began to examine nonprocreative types of sex and the people who perform them, which is key: it pathologized those who did not fit the normative model. Pedophilia, homosexuality, and extramarital sex got lumped together and came under the scrutiny of law and medicine. They became the subject of an entire matrix of discourse, which was kept in the hands of specialists by the taboos that prohibited "illegitimate" discourses about the subject. These various sexualities came to be labeled, classified, and defined. They became the constitutive Other by which normality was measured. Normality came to be defined as the lack of pathology, and as norms were defined, more pathologies were defined as well. They had to be. Pathologies are those phenomena to which the norm is opposed, and so the development of norms necessarily entails the concomitant development of pathology.

In a major shift in how sex and human experience were thought about, individual character replaced individual acts as the basis for how perversions were classified and described. When the act of sodomy came to be understood as a symptom of a kind of "interior androgyny,"[37] instead of a mere act anyone might perform, a category of person came to be: the homosexual was born. Once the homosexual began to be studied, a way to talk about the nonhomosexual was needed. Only then was the term "heterosexual" coined. In this peculiar conceptual arc, the homosexual existed before the heterosexual! It is this shift from act to character that opened the door to the arena of gender studies. Beauvoir and Foucault present serious challenges to the traditional conceptions of biological sex, sexuality, and gender as necessarily constitutive of one another. As they demonstrate, it is simply not the case that being born male or female will in every case cause an individual to manifest heterosexual attractions or exhibit typically masculine or feminine behaviors. And while medicine and biology have yielded a great deal of insight into how male and female bodies work, and psychology, sociology, and genetics have yielded some information on homosexuality, the relationship between personal identity and gender remained to be explored.

This is why Judith Butler's *Gender Trouble* has caused an enormous uproar in the fields of women's studies and gender studies since its publication in 1990. Butler's suggestion that gender is not essential but rather *performative* is revolutionary because it provides a new model for thinking gender that need not be seated in characteristics of bodies. Whereas Foucault examines the genesis of sexuality in Western thought and the operations of power on bodies, Butler examines the ways in which power is deployed to control the behavior of people and the performance of gender in the relationships that obtain between human beings. She believes that while gender is constitutive of identity, it is not fixed, stable, or substantive. She posits the notion of gender as a "complexity," never a whole, and never fully given. Gender is contingent on context, on culture, on situatedness—in short, on a myriad of specific, factical assemblages. Regulatory practices of gender govern identity, not the other way around. "In other words," Butler writes, "the 'coherence' and 'continuity' of 'the person' are not logical or analytic features of personhood, but, rather, socially instituted and maintained norms of intelligibility."[38] This is a very surprising thing to say, at first blush. However, it is consistent with contemporary trends regarding gender, and it is also compatible with the model of Dasein, as I demonstrate later. Butler was not the first to posit that gender is a social construction,[39] but she was the first to give a robust account of *how* gender is constructed. Gender studies today is a reaction to the premise of the constructionist model that Butler has initiated, and the various work in the field explores the consequences of what this means. The extent, details, and implications of constructionism are where most of the debate lies. While there certainly are plenty of people who are happy to critique Butler's theories, her performative theory of gender as a social construction remains the point of reference in a great deal of the current debates surrounding gender.

Setting the Table: Heidegger and Ontology

Although the issue of gender is such a muddle, a systematic examination of how gender is experienced can help to make sense of it, so phenomenology can do a lot of good for gender studies. This is by no means a definitive account of Heidegger's theory but rather a selective use of his model of Dasein in order to address the question of gender. Heidegger himself never did this; Dasein and his phenomenological method are well suited for this question because they allow the examination of what gets elided in traditional methods of study. Heidegger is the philosopher of the everyday; he set out to examine what gets taken for granted in human experience, what gets missed in its ubiquity. But-ler speaks of laying aside the notion of the coherent subject (or self) in order to understand gender as performative, experienced in everyday living. As it hap-pens, the model of Dasein is just such a means of discussing human experi-ence without presupposing a coherent subject and still remaining articulable. The subject may well not be a coherent, Cartesian unity or even a noun, but sentences still need subjects, and "Dasein" serves nicely.

In the early years of the twentieth century, Heidegger noticed a lacuna in the Western metaphysical tradition: the question of Being had been forgotten. The investigation into Being, into the wonder of the fact that Being persists, had been obscured by a tradition that occupied itself instead with entities, with less foundational questions and principles than what he saw as the most important—the investigation into that most universal, most self-evident, and therefore least-investigated phenomenon, *"the question of the meaning of Be-ing."*[40] This is no easy question to ask, since it amounts to questioning precisely what is presupposed in most inquiry, that the object of inquiry has some kind of Being. In *Being and Time*, Heidegger's aim is to formulate the question of Being in such a way that illuminates the conditions for the possibility of un-dertaking inquiry into entities. That is, Heidegger is interested in what he calls a more "primordial" question of how phenomena matter to people prior to investigations into scientific or metaphysical matters.[41]

To do this, Heidegger uses Dasein, the being to whom its own being mat-ters. Dasein is a model of human Being, but unlike most traditional philo-sophical models, which set out to identify the substances of which humans are composed, Dasein is characterized by its questioning and experiencing of its own Being. Heidegger claims that the "question of existence never gets straightened out except through existing itself."[42] It is through the process of Dasein's living and being meaningfully engaged in the world that the question of Being is established. The subject-object distinction[43] in traditional thinking is one Heidegger found to be problematic—such a distinction treats the hu-man being as the same kind of object as other entities and, in doing so, presup-poses certain characteristics instead of rigorously examining whether these characteristics obtain. Traditionally, the study of human nature approaches the subject, or the "I," as a fixed, stable, and substantive entity whose character can be delineated by definitions and which is distinct and separable (at least in the abstract) from the rest of the world. In short, the subject is traditionally assumed to be a mind observing the world at some distance. Dasein chal-lenges this model of subjecthood by presenting a being that is always already thrown into, or involved with, a world that is meaningful to it.[44] The world is incorporated into the fundamental Being of the entity to whom Being matters; Dasein's Being is its Being-in-the-world. Before the process of any formal or scholarly investigation can begin, Dasein is always already involved with the issue under investigation in a way that makes it evident that the issue matters to it. Indeed, Dasein studies that which is already meaningful to its life; if something does not matter, then Dasein does not have much reason for investigating it. (The study of medicine is not what makes life matter; rather, it is the fact that life matters that provides the motivation to study medicine.) It is helpful to think of Dasein less as a subject observing objects and more like that which experiences, as neither René Descartes's *res extensa* nor his *res cogitans* but more a process of the disclosure of entities and of the world. So no Dasein can be thought of as an entity that is distinct and separable from its historical context and involvement with the meaningfulness of its world, except in the most abstract sense that one can speak of the concept or model of Dasein. John Haugeland's explanation, that "a person is a case of Dasein"[45] in much the same way that spotty skin indicates a case of chicken pox, comes close. No single patient is the whole of chicken pox, but each case is a distinct manifestation of the disease and must receive individual treatment. So it is with Dasein: the individual is a manifestation of the particular kind of existence that experiences but is always also a particular manifestation and never an abstraction. Abstractions "flatten out" and erase difference, and Dasein is always its own particular specificity and is thus the essence of difference by being *this* particular way of being in *this* particular now.

The phenomenological method examines phenomena as Dasein experiences them, rather than seeking universal truths, which is the goal of traditional metaphysics. Subjective conscious experience is the starting point for phenomenology, and the goal is to gain insight into how phenomena experienced by Dasein are experienced at all and how they are relevant to Dasein's life. Appearance, which is discounted in traditional metaphysics and frequently regarded as an impediment to the pursuit of immutable truth, is the material under investigation in phenomenology. In this sense, Heidegger adopts the "principle of principles," Edmund Husserl's foundational point of origin:

> Every originary presentive intuition is a legitimizing source of cognition, that everything originarily (so to speak, in its "personal" actuality) offered to us in "intuition" is to be accepted simply as what it is presented as being, but also only within the limits in which it is presented there.[46]

This means that what Dasein experiences and how Dasein understands its experience are relevant topics of investigation to the phenomenologist. To contrast this with the metaphysical tradition, recall that in *Meditations on First Philosophy*, Descartes famously posited the idea that in the lack of clear and distinct certainty, all of reality might be a dream, and he concerned himself with how the "truth" of the matter might be discovered.[47] Were this notion of Descartes's to be proven, and were it settled once and for all that all human experience is illusion, perhaps the dream of some dozing god, the work of the phenomenologist still would not be finished. The experiences lived within the illusion are still important and worthy of investigation. The illusion itself would be a legitimate object of inquiry because it matters. To clarify the distinction and assist in articulating this concept, Heidegger distinguishes between the "ontical" and the "ontological." Both words are derived from the Greek *ontos*, "pertaining to being or existence," and together they express the distinction between kinds of being or experience. Ontical matters are details, the entities Dasein investigates in its dealings with the world, such as the scientific project to understand how things work in the world. The project of phenomenology, on the other hand, is ontological; it is concerned with gaining existential insight into the very context of the structures of existence itself.[48] By Heidegger's account, the foundational existential structures of Dasein's Being are its Being-in-the-world, care or concern for others, and temporality. That is, Dasein is characterized by its involvement with the world and with others, and with its plans for the future.

In addition, Dasein's Being-in-the-world is at any given time disclosed through mood, which is to say, it always already finds itself "in the mood that it has."[49] For instance, if an individual Dasein is frustrated, its Being is disclosed as the relationship between that which frustrates it (say, a broken chair) and that for the sake of which it is frustrated (Dasein itself, the work, and the plans it had for sitting in that chair). An entity that does not interfere with Dasein's plans (as a broken chair left out for the garbage) is not particularly likely to cause Dasein any frustration. Prior to taking an objective approach to any issue, Dasein is always already disposed to be meaningfully involved with the issue. It is this meaningful involvement that motivates Dasein to become objectively involved in the first place. Because Dasein matters, the work with the chair matters; because the work matters, the chair matters. Entities in the world, then, matter because they are part of what Heidegger calls a "totality of equipment"[50] within a context of meaningfulness; Dasein cares about them and is involved with them as equipment that aids or hinders the achievement of its goals. As long as equipment functions as it should, it is not the focus of Dasein's care but only a means to achieve the ends that Dasein does care about. It is *zuhanden*, or ready-to-hand, and is not significant in its own right but for the part it plays in the attainment of Dasein's goals. As long as this is the case, it goes largely unnoticed. But when equipment breaks down, it manifests itself as a hindrance to Dasein's goal, becoming conspicuous and thus a topic of investigation. It is now *vorhanden*, or present-at-hand, and is itself the object of Dasein's thought. Mood, then, is prior to objectivity; it is what makes engagement in objective inquiry meaningful.

This is no less the case when Dasein is involved with others in the world. Other cases of Dasein matter not as equipment but rather as the locus of meaningfulness of any individual's interaction with inanimate entities. Things are meaningful insofar as they are good for or bad for others as the recipients of Dasein's concern. So far as Dasein *is*, it is with-others, who are "there" along with Dasein (*Mitsein*, literally "Being-with" others). Dasein understands itself primarily as being involved in relationships with others and as part of a world inhabited by others, and for the most part these relationships occur within the public self that Heidegger calls *das Man*, or the "they." In statements like "They say one should use the salad fork with this course," the pronoun "they" refers to *das Man*. When Heidegger characterizes *das Man* as that "which supplies the answer to the question of *who* everyday Dasein is, is the *nobody* to whom Dasein has already surrendered itself in Being-with-one-another,"[51] he means that individuals generally define themselves in terms provided by *das Man*. Dasein mostly goes with the flow, just doing things as others do them until there is good reason to stop. It is through the public self of *das Man* that common patterns of understanding arise, forming norms and a basis on which each Dasein can understand itself in the average, everyday sense, and in comparison and contrast to which Dasein understands its own individuation and authenticity.

Everyday Dasein, the workaday self that is concerned with short-term goals and the general necessities of life, is what Heidegger calls "fallen" Dasein. Fallen Dasein is the they-self, the one who goes along with the normal way of doing things, as normality is understood by *das Man*. The description of fallenness in Heidegger's Dasein is richly articulated in the German term, *Uneigentlichkeit*, or unownedness, which is generally translated as "inauthenticity." Fallen Dasein does not "own" its experiences, in the full sense of the term, but rather accepts what is given as given and proceeds with its life in an unreflective manner. The term "fallen" offers some difficulty. Heidegger did not intend his use of the term to be a value judgment on fallen Dasein. It is not a bad thing for Dasein to be fallen. Rather, most of Dasein's life is lived in the fallen state. The fallen state is a comfortable state, in which Dasein need not take full responsibility for most aspects of its Being, which are determined by and understood in relation to *das Man*.

From time to time, however, Dasein's familiarity with the world gets disrupted and fails to operate as expected. At such times, Dasein's Being itself becomes conspicuous and an issue for reflective thinking. Dasein becomes preoccupied not with its short-term goals within a lived world but with its own place in this world as a whole. One phenomenon that precipitates this preoccupation is Dasein's understanding that it will die, which raises anxiety about its own Being.[52] Dasein understands its own Being as individuated from the enigmatic totality of *das Man* and as free to be meaningful on its own terms. At such times, Dasein *owns* its Being and experiences a moment of authenticity (*Eigentlichkeit*). Such moments are anxious, uncanny, and uncomfortable, as *das Man* does not and cannot provide an authentic, individuated Dasein with the script for how it is to proceed with its life. Anyone who has experienced a dry mouth and weak knees at a moment of taking a moral stand or a very big chance in life will recognize why this state of Being is both crucial and unpleasant. Authentic Dasein is faced with freedom to determine the course it will take in response to its own potentiality and the potentiality of the world, and it must make its own decisions on how to proceed with the process of living. Dasein is still very much in the world; this is not a mystical experience of altered reality but rather a difference in approach to Dasein's own life and freedom. Authentic Dasein takes responsibility for its own Being. The decisions it makes are infused with a significance that brings to light the wider range of possibilities inherent in the concerns of everyday existence. What Dasein takes responsibility *for* in acknowledging its own impending death is its own way of Being. Its life becomes its own. While there are cases of authentic Being-toward-death which have caused some individuals to drastically change their way of Being, such as Paul Gauguin, who gave up a wife and family to spend his life painting, in most cases the difference that authenticity makes in a life is not readily apparent. It applies more often to an attitude about life that is still lived in a seemingly ordinary manner. Religion illustrates this point: fallen Dasein merely accepts what it has been taught about the faith in which it has been raised and behaves accordingly. To approach faith authentically, Dasein must question religious doctrine and its meaningfulness for its own life. This does not mean that authentic Dasein is or is not religious, or that an authentic approach to religion necessarily requires a rejection of faith. It does mean that each Dasein must have asked questions and found answers that make pursuing that faith meaningful to its own life. In this way, Dasein can approach religion in an authentic manner.

Clearly, Heidegger's model of Dasein is a far cry from the traditional paradigm of a subject that experiences the world as something separate from itself.

The world and Dasein are not separate substances that can exist independently of one another. Certainly, without Dasein, entities are extant as "earth," but they are not a world; the world is that context of meaningfulness that arises through Dasein's involvement with entities. When one speaks of the "world" of science and the art "world," one is not naming distinctly different realities but, rather, distinctly different contexts of meaningfulness. Neither Dasein nor entities can be said to take priority in this involvement. Nor can it be said that any Dasein has Being independently of others; the world in which Dasein dwells necessarily involves others as considerations in its concern.

Heidegger's account raises the question of how Dasein can be an individual and also fundamentally *Mitsein* (Being-with). It might seem as though Heidegger might be establishing Dasein as a mere unit within a larger social self, but his case is more subtle than that. Dasein is a part of *das Man*, and its Being is *Mitsein*. "Resoluteness, as *authentic Being-one's-Self*, does not detach Dasein from its world, nor does it isolate it so that it becomes a free-floating 'I.' And how should it, when resoluteness as authentic disclosedness, is *authentically* nothing other than *Being-in-the-world*?"[53] That is, fallen Dasein is the they-self and does not take responsibility for its own choices in the way that authentic Dasein does. In individuating, however, Dasein becomes "its own" and faces its own finitude as an "I," an individual who is ontologically differentiated from fallen Dasein.[54] This means that there is something that Dasein is but that this something is not to be thought of as a thing or an object separate from the public experience of Dasein—it *is* public experience, *this* particular causal chain of experience rather than *that* causal chain over there. The self that maintains its identity throughout experiences in the world, and yet is neither a stable whole nor a manifold of experience, operates like this: Dasein's "'*substance*' is not spirit as a synthesis of soul and body; it is rather *existence*."[55] Each Dasein is its facticity, which is to say that each individual Dasein is a particular instance of existence that occurs within the larger whole of a community or of humanity itself. The continuity of the individual's experiences over the span of a lifetime is what ties the identity of a given Dasein together into an "I." At the same time, the way an individual Dasein understands these experiences is always already within a world established by *das Man*.

Now, since each case of Dasein is both *Mitsein* and an individual, acts of individuation are a matter of balancing tension between the they-self and the authentic self. By Heidegger's account, the primary motivator for Dasein's authentic individuation is anxiety in the face of its own impending death. Anxiety at the understanding that its own Being will end creates a conflict between the they-self and Dasein's potentiality for authenticity, which incites

Dasein to evaluate its life as something present-at-hand, as something to be evaluated as distinct from the comfortable everydayness of *das Man*. Anxiety in the face of death is the mood that most clearly and painfully makes evident to Dasein that its own death is unique and that it cannot be substituted by the death of another. In this sense, death is always "mine" and never "ours"; it is the impending ceasing of the "Being-there" that Dasein is and, as such, has the capacity to disclose Dasein's Being to it, by contrasting it with the impending not-Being of its very self. Heidegger's account is correct, as far as it goes: anxiety is the *primary* existential structure of Dasein's individuation, but I do not believe that anxiety in the face of death is the *only* mood that has the capacity to disclose Dasein's Being. This is evidenced by the fact that other kinds of conflict do exist, including the uncanniness brought about by some individuals' failure to conform to social norms, which has the capacity to bring about an authentic evaluation of those lives and thus contributes to Dasein's individuation.

My position is that Heidegger's account of anxiety is correct but not exhaustive; there is a rich vein of thought to be explored in the discovery of other disclosive phenomena, not least of which is gender. In "What Is Metaphysics?" he does hint that love and boredom are emotional states capable of disclosing Being to Dasein,[56] which suggests that his own focus on death is aimed at giving a robust account of *one* disclosive phenomenon rather than privileging anxiety in the face of death as *the* disclosive phenomenon. Furthermore, in *Being and Time*, he makes reference to Leo Tolstoy's *The Death of Ivan Ilych*[57] as an example of a case in which a character is individuated by death, to be sure, but is also individuated prior to his death by his state of physical disability, which causes him to no longer "fit in" with *das Man* and to become an annoyance to others. Boredom, love, and disability, then, are also phenomena that have the potential to bring about authentic individuation, and so my assertion that gender transgression is a phenomenon that shares this potential is not a radical departure from Heidegger's account of anxiety in the face of death. Rather, it is a new application of his method to an underexplored aspect of Dasein's Being.

To tie this all together, Dasein is its specificity, its historicity, and its facticity. But Dasein is also *Mitsein* and *das Man*. And *Mitsein* and *das Man* are characterized by their historical and geographic locations but are also precisely what is not specific and factical but rather general and a totality. Dasein (and especially authentic Dasein) is a being that is meaningfully involved in negotiating the tensions that obtain between its specificity and its participation in a totality, forging its own life out of the potentialities afforded by both aspects of its Being. It is the case that within any community, different members will occupy different roles, even to the point of forming different types of people and thus genders (*Geschlechten*), which results in conflicts of interest among members of a community.[58] No culture or community is entirely uniform, and even within relatively homogeneous cultures, different individuals occupy different social roles, and such differences necessitate that there is conflict among the cases of Dasein who constitute *das Man*. As Dorothy Leland points out,

> When the norms articulated by *das Man* largely express the sense of what is important, what is possible, and what is permissible for dominant social groups, and when these norms conflict with or suppress alternative interpretations, leveling down also occurs as a suppression of alternatives expressed in marginalized stories and practices that contest the dominant culture.[59]

Each Dasein, as an individual, is uniquely oriented in-the-world, and this orientation affects the potentiality of each Dasein's Being. A particular Dasein may find itself born into an impoverished family or as a wealthy heir; one Dasein may possess features that conform to standards of beauty, while another does not. In each case, the factical details of the way Dasein finds itself oriented have an effect on its potentiality for Being-in-the-world and the shape that its ownmost potentiality for Being may take. The lack of alterity in Heidegger's description of *das Man* overlooks how fallenness may contribute to the oppression of those who do not belong to dominant groups by simply disregarding or glossing over their existence. It also overlooks the potential for Dasein to be individuated or singled out by virtue of its failing to conform to the expectations and presuppositions of *das Man*. Transgressive individuals are cast from the fold and thus forced to confront a unique orientation in-the-world as a consequence of social disapprobation or disregard. But *das Man* is never a pure phenomenon, and no Dasein can ever fully conform to *das Man* in every aspect of its life. The tension between Dasein's specificity and the degree to which it participates in *das Man* is a source of constant pressure and is particularly conspicuous in cases of some individuals' being oppressed by the dominant stances of any given social sphere.

Kevin Aho presents an interesting perspective on the debate regarding Dasein's gender neutrality, by factoring Dasein's temporality into the question of gender. On Heidegger's account, Dasein's temporality is part of its foundational existential nature; the way Dasein experiences time is crucial to the way Dasein understands the world. Aho's thesis is that whatever the actual gendered practices of any Dasein or any community of *das Man* may be, there is a commonality among all: that Dasein is always projected, or thrown, out of its past and into a future. Any involvement with the world, and the intelligibility of that world, happens within a kind of "primordial time," which is always understood as a span, rather than a series of moments, shaped by the experience of the past and the anticipation of the future. Aho writes,

> Fundamental ontology is primarily concerned with the conditions that make the world meaningful, allowing things to show up *as* such and such. And it is *not* by means of my present involvement in the world that things make sense to me. The world is meaningful because, as I invariably press forward into social possibilities, I am thrown back into a public situation where things already count and matter to me.[60]

So, in this respect, on Aho's reading Dasein can be said to be gender neutral: all instances of Dasein, regardless of biology, social role, or personal identity share this temporality of Being. By means of this temporal structure, Dasein has the capacity not only to reiterate the presuppositions of *das Man* but also to recognize them as contingent and factical, rather than essential to gender itself, precisely because primordial temporality creates the conditions under which Dasein's Being can be examined. Aho maintains, then, that temporality is a more primordial facet of Dasein's Being than *Mitsein* or *das Man*, and it is in this sense that Heidegger posits Dasein as being gender neutral.

I disagree. Dasein is, to be sure, always engaged in thrown projection out of its past and into its future, but this thrown projection is always already thrown projection *of* some experiences. And these experiences are, by necessity, experiences of other equiprimordial structures such as *das Man*, understanding, and historical situatedness, all of which entail gender. Aho's characterization of Heidegger's model of temporal Dasein as gender neutral may pose a challenge to essentialist accounts of gender, by allowing the understanding that neither biological nor metaphysical determinism is at work in Dasein's temporal disposition. All cases of Dasein, regardless of biology, have temporal thrownness in common. But his account does not undermine a constructionist understanding of gender, which holds that gender is a social construction and contingent but also regulatory of Dasein's ownmost potentiality for Being. The concerns with which Dasein is engaged in its temporal dispositions arise out of the social sphere in which Dasein always already finds itself, and this social sphere is always one in which the constant tension between Dasein's specificity and its participation in *das Man* is a concern. Thus, Dasein is never a common denominator of all humanity or a Platonic form of human-being-ness. Dasein is rather always already actively concerned with alterity and conformity, with what is not neutral and not universal as regards itself and its projections into the future. Thus, gendered concerns are the stuff of which temporal concerns are made. Indeed, because it is public, *das Man* is "insensitive to every difference of level and genuineness. . . . By publicness everything gets obscured, and what has thus been covered up gets passed off as something familiar and accessible to everyone."[61] What is obscured is the ever-present tension between Dasein's they-self and its specificity, and in some cases this tension can interfere with Dasein's fallenness and force Dasein into anxiety in the face of not death but uncanniness, a sense of not fitting in or not being at home, which has the potential to force authentic disclosure of Dasein's ownmost possibility for being in a way that is transgressive of *das Man*'s expectations.

Since *Mitsein* is not a homogeneous whole, various cases of Dasein are divided into types and have their own individual orientations that shape their ownmost potentiality for Being. So there will always be ways of dividing individuals up within *das Man*, and there will thus always be the questions that drive this project of the question of gender (*Geschlecht*). To be sure, the tendency of *das Man* to be divided in terms of sexual difference and gender, however ubiquitous, is contingent. The two are conceptually linked by specific historical traditions of medicine, politics, religion, and so on. But this is a contingency grounded in the primordial phenomenon of *das Man*'s heterogeneous structure, which is simply a consequence of *das Man*'s being composed of many individuals with individual orientations. The linking of gender with sexual difference that generates expectations regarding behaviors (which is urgent in our culture and our time but may not be as urgent in another time) is thus disclosive of this more primordial, heterogeneous structure of *das Man*, a structure of constant tension and flux that plays out in the specificity of each Dasein's orientation and participation in *das Man*.

Heidegger's account of Dasein and world has also been accused of reducing relationships to equipmental ones. Things in the world are either *zuhanden* or *vorhanden*, and there are no other options presented. But is human Being not richer than this? Where do emotional relationships fit into this scheme? What about abhorrence or delight? An arachnophobic Dasein might find its plans thwarted by the presence of a spider in its workspace, but is there not more than disruption of goals at work in such a case? Are not fear and aversion in the face of spiders themselves phenomena that constitute this particular Dasein's Being? Heidegger characterizes fear as something that "discloses Dasein predominantly in a privative way. It bewilders us and makes us 'lose our heads.' Fear closes off endangered Being-in, and yet at the same time lets us see it, so that when the fear has subsided, Dasein must first find its way about again."[62] So fear discloses the world that is normally taken for granted by violating ordinary everydayness and causes Dasein to step out of itself temporarily. It seems delight might operate in a similar way, causing Dasein to "lose its head," immersing itself in delight, in something other than ordinary everydayness. The difference is that Dasein seeks to avoid that which it fears and seeks to experience that in which it delights. In both cases, however, Dasein is *orienting* itself away from or toward certain phenomena. Dasein not only finds itself always already oriented in the world in some particular, factical way or other but also actively participates in this orientation as it goes about its life. In seeking that which is delightful and avoiding that which is fearsome, Dasein involves itself not in a world that is reducible to mere equipmentality but rather in one in which pleasure is sought and pains avoided for the sake of pleasure itself and not some other end. And, since Dasein finds more pleasure in some aspects of the world, it orients itself accordingly, and so the act of orientation is an individuating act on Dasein's part.

Now, for the most part, Dasein's orientation, while individuating, is inauthentic; Dasein generally seeks to remain fallen in *das Man* most of the time. And why should it not? Authenticity is painful and difficult, disclosive as it is of Dasein's Being. It is sometimes rewarding, but there is no guarantee that it will be. So what can be powerful enough to motivate unwilling individuals toward authenticity? Anxiety in the face of one's own unique death is one answer, but the uncanniness that is triggered by anxiety is not unique to Being-toward-death. At times, some find themselves so oriented in-the-world as to be in conflict with the expectations of *das Man*, and this too can bring about anxiety and uncanniness. Being different or strange makes people uncomfortable and makes the points of difference from others very conspicuous indeed. The causes of difference may be known or unknown, but the phenomenon is common enough that this much can be said: some Dasein are so constituted or oriented as to be inclined to avoid that in which most delight or to seek out that which most avoid. This too is a site of alterity within *das Man*, as different members of the community, oriented in different directions, seek to satisfy differing or even conflicting interests. And those who find that their interests are in conflict with *das Man* itself, and who, with the expectations *das Man* places on them, may well find themselves in a situation in which fallenness, blending in, simply is not available to them, are excluded by *das Man*. In such a case, Dasein has no choice to flee into fallenness but simply must face its life as something *vorhanden*, as something to be examined. In such a case, the choice Dasein faces is not one of fallenness versus authenticity but rather to

(1) live as an abjected outsider, (2) die, or (3) take charge of its life and own it in an authentic manner. There is no guarantee that transgression leads to authenticity, of course, but there is a possibility of their concomitance.

Uncanniness can arise at any time or in any way Dasein strikes out on its own and transgresses the habits and expectations of *das Man*. Indeed, any time Dasein invents or innovates, some sort of transgression of norms occurs, and it would be odd indeed to characterize all such transgression of norms as always being motivated by the same anxiety in the face of death. The invention of the light bulb transgressed the norm of using oil lamps for light and helped to put an end to the preeminence of the whaling industry. No less do inventions or innovations in the social sphere transgress established norms. This can happen as a result of changes to the equipmental relationship to entities in the world but also in response to emotions regarding entities and other cases of Dasein, such as when a transgender individual "comes out of the closet," rejecting the invisibility, along with all its concomitant misery, demanded by *das Man* of those who are of transgressive orientations. Now, since at times the fallen state is impossible for some individuals to achieve, or is intolerable, or simply has room for improvement, motivation arises to make a change of one kind or another in an individual's manner of Being. Such changes are always a transgression of some kind of norm. And it is *das Man* that establishes norms, so such transgression is one step on the way to authenticity, to resolutely owning a facticity that cannot simply fade into the background.

Applied Ontology and How It Works

The hard sciences are generally understood as being empirical investigations concerned with observations and discovery of facts. As such, they are ontical investigations. Within the sciences, a further distinction can be made between those sciences that are concerned with "hard facts," such as physics, and those that are referred to as "arts," such as medicine. The former are reliant on logical conclusions regarding observation of the natural world, whereas the latter are reliant on observation and technology and at the same time intrinsically involved with the ontological essence of Being, in that they are committed to preserving and improving the conditions of that Being. The aim of medicine is to improve and extend life, which means that ontological presuppositions regarding the essence of life and death lay at the heart of the science of medicine.[63] The art of medicine is practiced as a response to the anxiety felt in the face of death, the end of the Being of any Dasein, and is thus not an ontological inquiry but nevertheless *involved with* ontological concerns.

This book aims to provide an *application* of the theories Heidegger developed in his fundamental ontology to the lived human experience of gender, the particular details of which in any given situation are ontical. For all the value of the natural sciences, and there is great value indeed, there are questions to be asked about human experiences that the sciences do not address. Furthermore, the sciences do not provide the best methodology for every inquiry. Biology and psychology, for instance, are limited in their scope to specific kinds of fact and do not address the meaningfulness that makes these facts worth the time and trouble of gathering and interpreting. These disciplines tell a great deal about how bodies and minds operate, but they cannot tell what presuppositions biology and psychology are burdened with from the start; nor do they establish why anyone should care. Similarly, medical experts can tell whether a newborn is male, female, or intersex, but the medical understanding of biological sex is a far cry from the way gender is meaningful in lived experience. To examine the presuppositions and classificatory systems employed in the sciences, and to understand how Dasein experiences them, ontology is the proper method of inquiry. This kind of applied ontology, then, is the examination of the foundations of the positive sciences, including medicine, psychology, anthropology, and sociology, and of the presuppositions that drive and shape scientific inquiry. One could say that applied ontology "follows through" on scientific inquiry, with the aim of understanding the most basic and primordial ways in which scientific inquiry is meaningful to human life.[64] In this sense, the question of gender is no mere history of gender difference but rather an ontological question, in that it is concerned with the ways in which gender affects and is affected by Dasein's Being-in-the-world.

A great deal of gender theory focuses on ontical questions of applied ethics rather than on the ontological question of how Dasein *experiences* gender and how gender is foundational to Dasein's Being.[65] This is because the issue of gender generally becomes conspicuous as an issue precisely when there are problems associated with it. In very broad terms, the method employed by applied ethics can be characterized as a process of identifying particular issues of moral import or contention and addressing what ought to be done about them. This identification is frequently predicated on suffering; ethical issues come to light because there is a problem for some of those involved, and the utility, rights, duties, and virtues involved are evaluated. The women's movement, the civil rights movement, and the gay rights movements have all occurred because oppression became conspicuous, and they have served to address these problems and attempted to fix them. This method has had some success in relieving human suffering, particularly in the past two centuries.

At the same time, however, these issues of moral import have their origin not in the ethical debates regarding those who are suffering but rather in Dasein's very Being, in the stories Dasein tells, in the presuppositions that shape Dasein's inquiries, and in the particular circumstances in which Dasein finds itself.

Given the urgency of the issue of gender in the West at this time, this focus on applied ethics and political equality is not surprising. At the same time, it is clear that a well-grounded applied ontology is needed if ethical and political claims are to be justifiable.[66] To put it bluntly, we need to understand how gender is experienced for all before we can determine what, if anything, to do *about* it in the case of transgressors. Applied ontology provides the means for articulating the difficulties faced in the field as a whole and for informing the premises on which ethical prescriptions can be established. The philosophical tradition elides gender difference, rather than creating ideal conditions for scrutinizing it, and risks universalizing claims about gender, which fails to address the issues relevant to all. This leaves some unaccounted for, thus perpetuating the very injustices that the inquiry was meant to correct. As an example, Judith Butler's groundbreaking *Gender Trouble* notes that feminist philosophies frequently adopt the philosophical tradition's presupposition of a coherent subject. This serves to reinscribe the universality of patriarchal systems, which universalize the masculine and exclude the feminine.[67] This is one description of tradition eliding difference, but it does not stop there. In turn, Butler's own performative theory was initially misread by some as being an argument that gender is a choice made by a coherent subject, that gender could be assumed or discarded at will, like clothing.[68] The reason for this misreading is that the philosophical tradition has very little means at its disposal for articulating the concept of performance without a conscious, willing performer—that is, a coherent subject.[69] The error came about because Butler's work was read as being *within* rather than *against* the philosophical tradition, so her theory was mistaken for a claim that would exclude those who do not experience gender as being a matter of choice or will. As this example demonstrates, it can be very difficult to articulate challenges to traditional presuppositions because those challenges are read against a backdrop that consists of the same presuppositions they challenge. This is a pitfall that can be avoided, but it is not easy and often means writing sentences that do not, at first, seem to make sense.

As with any social movement, a great many of the voices are of those most deeply invested in the questions that drive the movement. In the case of gender theory, those voices are of gender transgressive individuals telling our stories and thus bringing the issue of gender into the spotlight as an issue that must be addressed. The question of what can be done to relieve suffering is the logical consequence of hearing such stories, but it is not the only consequence that is needed. In addition to this, a means of linking understanding of what *is* to what *ought to be* is called for. Asking the question of gender has the potential to do more than relieve suffering; it has the power to prevent the occasion for suffering by providing insight into the ways problems arise in the first place, and thus to avoid merely treating symptoms of ethical concern and instead address the causes.

Three themes in Heidegger's work come to light as being of particular interest to feminist thinkers and gender theorists alike: embodiment, alterity, and innovation. The first is a bit ironic, if understandable, given Heidegger's critique of Western metaphysics as having left the question of Being unasked. There are themes on which Heidegger himself remains relatively silent, not least of which is the issue of embodiment and sexual difference. As a consequence, some have suggested that Heidegger may be guilty of failing to take into consideration the very real effects that embodiment and sexual difference have on Dasein's factical Being and thus leaving his theories open to criticisms, such as Tina Chanter's suggestion that "Heidegger's account of Dasein remains more consonant with the disembodied transcendental subject that Heidegger claims Kant inherited from Descartes than Heidegger admits."[70]

The second theme, alterity, is related to the first. Although Heidegger never developed an ethical theory, his ontology does raise important ethical questions. How are Dasein's obligations to be understood in light of its historicity, facticity, thrownness, and *Mitsein*? How is it that Dasein's world is constituted and meaningful, and what limitations does this place on Dasein's freedom? There may be a contradiction among Heidegger's account of Dasein as Being-in-the-world, his account of Dasein as foundationally *Mitsein*, and his account of authenticity. Dasein's state, in its ordinary everydayness, is one of concern toward others. But if Dasein is to become individuated and to own its own Being, thereby achieving "coherence, cohesiveness, and integrity [in] a life course,"[71] then it must, at least temporarily, become *un*concerned with others. The implications of such a contradiction create an interesting conundrum.

Heidegger gives an account of how it is that *das Man*, or "the They," constitutes social convention and cultural context, thus acting as the guiding force in Dasein's life insofar as Dasein is "fallen" and "inauthentic."[72] What he does not give an account of is the fact that there must be internal divisions within *das Man*. As Leland notes, all members of a culture or community have some kind of common intelligibility, but there inevitably also are conflicting points of view regarding goals, possibilities, and desires.[73] Those at the higher end of the socioeconomic range will not have the same aspirations and goals as those at the lower ends. In addition, those who are in a position of dominance are also in a position to influence the values of the community, thus devaluing the lived experience of more subordinate members.[74] This observation has obvious implications for the fields of women's studies and gender studies, since women and those who do not conform to gender expectations are almost always to be found in the position of subordination. A fresh evaluation of gender on the part of phenomenology addresses the third theme, innovation, as these ideas have the power to change the way gender is thought from its core and understand the world in which all dwell.

There is, then, a great deal of work still to be done in the area of Heidegger's thought and gender studies. This book is only a small part of that work. On one hand, Western culture's deep investment in gender norms and their perpetuation is exemplified in the threats and performance of violence against those who violate gender norms; it seems that some consider the maintenance of social norms regarding gender as having priority over the rights or even the lives of human beings, children included. On the other hand, Western culture is also deeply invested in valuing individuality and avoiding suffering wherever possible. It is clear that some individuals do not fit gender norms, that suffering results from nonconformity, and that the apparent contradiction between these investments demands attention. This text is not intended to offer an explicit ethical or political agenda. It is clear, however, that the potential ethical ramifications of an ontology of gender intersect with the issues addressed by applied ethicists. In factical life, ontology and ethics are not sharply delineated areas of specialty. Since gender is significant both as a facet of personal identity and as the inscription of cultural norms, there is a great deal of ethical and political weight involved in any examination of the relationships between nature and culture. My aim with this book is more to describe than to prescribe, although it must be admitted that descriptions lead to prescriptions. What I explicitly wish to avoid is anything that smacks of a manifesto to map out what the future world ought to be. That would be a mistake that repeats the very kind of intolerance for cultural innovation that is displayed by those who react violently to gender nonconformists.

So just what is it that Heidegger's phenomenology brings to the table? To sum up, Heidegger makes a seismic shift in thinking that manages to avoid the traditional problems of metaphysics, which snarl themselves in logical puzzles about identity. The shift from questions of substance and the nature of the self to descriptions of everyday experience allows discussion of experience as it is lived, which permits a much wider range of lived truth to enter discussions without dismissing the unknown or unspoken as incoherent or having to account for rigid universals. Particularity is not a problem for the phenomenologist, and contingency enriches discussion.

In the academy, it is clear that any discussion of social construction is highly dependent on intersectionality—gender is lived differently by members of different social classes and members of different races, for instance. None of these social technologies operates in a vacuum; they are always experienced and lived in concert with one another as overlapping communities. This awareness is passing from the academy to the consciousness of the general public, eliciting varying degrees of bafflement and delight: delight because intersectionality is a key component of highlighting previously unappreciated experience and bafflement because conversations about social technologies are getting difficult to hold with the language most people use. It is true that there will always be something omitted, some aspect of experience not given full voice. Any discussion of experience, particularly among marginalized groups, glosses over some crucial aspect of any group's facticity. A discussion of the experience of a specific white transsexual man necessarily omits the perspectives of trans women of color. Any discussion of transsexuality as such might thus seem to be tasked with incorporating differing experiences into the conversation to gain a well-rounded understanding of transsexuality. But it is not. Intersectionality reveals a crucial truth: that any account of lived experience is of necessity partial, and to gain a well-rounded understanding, it is necessary to engage with many different accounts and perspectives.[75] The phenomenologist's humility is hereby employed to gain as varied an understanding as possible, while leaving the search for universals to metaphysicians.

Ontology is such a valuable tool for examining what matters precisely because it manages to sidestep some of the difficulties raised by traditional metaphysical accounts of what humans are. Instead of focusing on theories of the self or identity puzzles, Heidegger shifts attention to the phenomena of human experience. Dasein is not a thing. It is the condition of Being-there, and the "there" into which Dasein is thrown is always a complex intersection of phenomena. In the pages that follow, I sometimes use the term almost synonymously with "individual" in the grammatical sense, but the value in the word is to disrupt the notion of self-as-substance that we are so accustomed to in Western thinking, to serve as a reminder that it is Dasein's thrownness and performance that are at stake in this discussion.

Debate might abound about the reality and substance and nature of my pen, but the experience I have of writing with the pen is indubitable; questioning whether the experience is real would be nonsensical. According to Husserl's principle of principles, what is experienced is legitimately an object of inquiry, and appearance matters. Take the recent controversy over a photograph of a dress that some people see as white and gold and others see as blue and black.[76] There is no "correct" or "incorrect" perception of the dress, even though some individuals' perceptions might change if they were to see the same dress in a different photograph or under different light. The perception itself remains exactly what it is, a perception, and the perceiver is the one who "is there," Dasein. The discussion gets interesting when the reasons for differing perceptions are examined. How we perceive the world is important, and it is crucial to recognize that not everyone's perceptions are the same. There are good reasons that different Dasein have different perceptions; they are at different points of intersection. Perception drives action, behavior, and valuing, literally shaping life itself, and at times an understanding of others' perception is crucial to informing one's own.

When thinkers use a nonphenomenological approach, a conversation about a social construction can all too easily disregard crucial facets that must be approached intersectionally. A discussion of, say, transsexuality cannot make much sense if the concept of transsexuality is divorced from age, race, class, ability, and so on. All of these issues' influence on one another are too important to disregard, and thus traditional metaphysical commitments to universals and essentialisms make it very difficult to discuss any intersectional nexus. When some things are said, other things are left unsaid. Exceptions are not just difficult to avoid; they are inevitable. This creates a puzzle that demands solution, especially since to not speak is also to make a statement, to erase what is left unspoken. As long as such discussions are reliant on essentialist theories of personal identity and abstract universals, they will fail in various, often crucial, ways to address the lived experience of some members of any given community.[77] And this is why the methods Heidegger uses are so valuable—in positing Dasein as its facticity, as what it experiences, in *this* place and in *this* time, we can discuss social technologies as experiences without the necessity of excluding members of community. Applied ontology avoids treating identity as though it is a possession of a discrete subject, a thing distinct from the world in which it dwells. This is a type of predicate error; Dasein's identity is not the same kind of thing as a possession, and Dasein is not distinct from its lived world. The only way for Dasein to Be is as an entity always already involved in a context rich with identifying phenomena. Dasein's identity is not a possession but rather a direction of attention and activity, an intentional stance within overlapping contexts that make up a meaningful world. Take "The Question Concerning Technology" as an example. In isolating the phenomenon of technology for discussion, Heidegger avoids the necessity of privileging one part of the community's perspective or experience of technology over that of another part of the community. He does not distinguish between kinds of people but sticks to the way technology is employed and experienced. Yet all Dasein are "technological" in various ways. On Heidegger's account, technology is a world-shaping phenomenon, an ordering and disclosive worldview. As I have written elsewhere,

> Technology allows us to understand the world at all, to articulate our particular, factical experience, which is always anomalous and never simply a type. (Particulars are always anomalies; there is always something to distinguish this instance of any thing from its type.) We must have some way of making sense of our experiences, and this tension between what we are and what we are at any moment becoming creates the circumstances under which change occurs and new ways of being-human come to light.[78]

When combined with Heidegger's conception of technology, Foucault's conception of "technologies of the self" makes it clear that social constructions, too, operate as technologies.[79] Heidegger draws a broad picture of *Mitsein* and the enormous influence of concern in human life. On my reading, Foucault zooms in on that broader map of experience, describing the particulars of how a given course of history has brought specific communities to the place in which they find themselves at a distinct time. He reasons from the broadly ontological to the narrowly ontical and then back again, examining the particular operations of the phenomena Heidegger sketches and then illustrating how the conduits of power are constructed. Viewing the individual perpetuation of normative discourses through disciplinary applications of power side by side with the understanding of technology as disclosive of worldview opens up the notion of social constructions as technologies with which human beings are actively and productively engaged, whether consciously or not. The first and most important step is to recognize social constructions *as* technologies, as opposed to metaphysical truths. This already involves a shift in perspective, placing social constructions in a *vorhanden* position to be observed and affected by the very members of the community who are perpetuating them. Power shapes us, but we collectively shape the institutions that exert power on us, as well. The complex systems and intersections of power are never static; they are constantly updated and repurposed in factical life.

While his account of technology is certainly of Heidegger's time and perspective, disclosing aspects of human experience, it is never posited as *the* account of technology or a way to box up a particular type of person for popular consumption. The isolation from other aspects of experience is certainly an artifice that abstracts that experience from the intersectional ways in which it is actually lived, but it is an abstraction of *the phenomenon*, not an abstraction of persons into types. This is important; it focuses on listening to how people (as Dasein) experience phenomena, instead of distilling individuals or human experience into abstractions, and leaves the field open for tinkering by those who are most intimately concerned with that experience. Technologies shape individuals, and at the same time, the concerns of individuals shape technology. This is a crude way to put it; no doubt the concept still needs refining, but an approach to social constructions as technologies may help with the puzzle of how to discuss the ways in which some members of a community are failed by that community's social technologies without excluding other marginalized members of the community. It avoids the erasure of the other that is the natural consequence of isolating one part of a community for attention to the exclusion of others.

This is not to say that employing applied ontology as a method to examine social technologies does not entail exclusion. But it is not *people* who are excluded from the discussion. In Western thinking, the traditional distinctions between mind and body, and between self and world, drive the identity-based approach to matters of marginalization, which lies at the heart of the enframing of people into essential types that are rendered increasingly more rigid by social convention. When, on the other hand, what is experienced is legitimately an object of inquiry and appearance matters, when there is no "correct" or "incorrect" perception of a phenomenon, the question of what is to be done about injustices shifts from one of personal type to one of shared social project. Confrontation between wounded community members may (*may!*) be replaced with cooperative endeavor, affecting the way we ask questions in the sciences, ethics, and metaphysics. The acceptance of varying perception, of Dasein's facticity in all its diverse splendor, allows variance in action, behavior, and valuing. It literally shapes the world differently.

Notes

1. Jeffrey Eugenides, *Middlesex* (New York: Farrar, Straus and Giroux, 2002), 446.

2. Hanna Rosin, "A Boy's Life," *The Atlantic*, November 2008, http://theatlantic.com/doc/200811/transgender-children; Robbie Brown, "Transgender Candidate Who Ran as Woman Did Not Mislead Voters, Court Says," *New York Times*, October 6, 2008, http://www.nytimes.com/2008/10/07/us/07gender.html; Michelle Garcia, "School District Mum on Trans Teacher," *The Advocate*, October 17, 2008, http://www.advocate.com/news/2008/10/17/school-district-mum-trans-teacher.

3. Whether because of increased incidents or because of increased coverage of incidents, there has been an increase in news reports of children as young as seventeen months being killed because of perceived transgression of gender norms. In every one of these cases, nonthreatening, gender-variant behavior has been met with deadly force. Erin Hartness, "Cult-like Group Behaviors Come out in Court," *WRAL*, October 18, 2011, http://www.wral.com/news/local/story/9836148/; Catherine Saillant, "Teen in Gay-Student Slaying Case Agrees to 21-Year Prison Term," *Los Angeles Times*, November 21, 2011, http://latimesblogs.latimes.com/lanow/2011/11/gay-slaying.html; Josh Einiger, "Man Indicted in Shinnecock Baby Death" *ABC News*, August 11, 2010, http://abclocal.go.com/wabc/story?section=news/local&id=7605381.

4. Martin Heidegger, *Being and Time*, trans. John Macquarrie and Edward Robinson (San Francisco: HarperCollins, 1962), 29; H. 9. Page numbers preceded by "H." refer to pages in the original German work, Martin Heidegger, *Sein und Zeit* (Tübingen, Germany: Max Niemeyer Verlag, 1927).

5. Ibid., 32; H. 12.

6. Ibid., 67; H. 42.

7. See Hubert Dreyfus's explication of "disharmonies," especially in Charles Spinosa, Fernando Flores, and Hubert L. Dreyfus, *Disclosing New Worlds: Entrepreneurship, Democratic Action, and the Cultivation of Solidarity* (Cambridge, MA: MIT Press, 1997).

8. Heidegger, *Being and Time*, 44; H. 22.

9. See Judith Butler, "Doing Justice to Someone: Sex Reassignment and Allegories of Transsexuality," in *Undoing Gender* (New York: Routledge, 2004), 57–74. Butler does address issues such as the livability of a life, but her work in this area primarily focuses on applied ethics, not an applied ontology.

10. John W. Hole, Jr., *Human Anatomy and Physiology* (Dubuque, IA: Wm. C. Brown, 1978), 712, 721.

11. Intersex Society of North America, "How Common Is Intersex?" http://www.isna.org/faq/frequency (accessed January 20, 2017). The statistic cited here is an estimate because some intersex conditions are not readily identifiable.

12. Anne Fausto-Sterling, *Sexing the Body: Gender Politics and the Construction of Sexuality* (New York: Basic Books, 2000), 44–45.

13. See American Psychological Association, "Answers to Your Questions about Individuals with Intersex Conditions," 2006, http://www.apa.org/topics/lgbt/intersex.aspx; and Intersex Society of North America, "Our Mission," http://www.isna.org/ (accessed January 20, 2017).

14. See Sigmund Freud, "The Sexual Aberrations," in *Three Essays on the Theory of Sexuality*, ed. and trans. James Strachey (New York: Basic Books, 2000), 1–38.

15. American Psychiatric Association, *Diagnostic and Statistical Manual of Mental Disorders*, 5th ed. (Arlington, VA: American Psychiatric Association, 2013), 302.3.

16. "Cisgender" is a frequently used neologism that combines the prefix "cis-," which means "on the same side," with the term "gender" and indicates that gender identity is in accordance with biological sex, with regard to the standards set by cultural, legal, medical, and social expectations. Cisgender men, for instance, are biologically male, masculine gendered, and find there to be no incongruity between their gender identity and their biological sex. The term is in use and refers to individuals who are not transgender. The coining of the term is attributed to Carl Buijs, "A New Perspective on an Old Topic"

thread, *Soc.support.transgendered*, April 16, 1996, http://groups.google.com/group/soc .support.transgendered/msg/18485odf15e48963?hl=en.

17. Judith Butler, *Gender Trouble: Feminism and the Subversion of Identity* (New York: Routledge, 1990), 11.

18. India's *hijras* and Thailand's toms and dees are examples of this phenomenon.

19. This holds, whether this standard is the statistical norm or not. At times, cultural norms are more aspirational than descriptive, as with the American Dream, which holds all Americans to a standard of middle-class prosperity even in the face of a precipitously widening wealth gap.

20. Thomas Beatie, "Labor of Love," *The Advocate*, March 14, 2008, http://www.advo cate.com/news/2008/03/14/labor-love.

21. Alan B. Goldberg and Katie N. Thomson, "Barbara Walters Exclusive: Pregnant Man Expecting Second Child," *ABC News*, November 13, 2008, http://abcnews.go.com/ Health/Story?id=6244878.

22. Thomas Rogers, "What the Pregnant Man Didn't Deliver," *Salon*, July 3, 2008, http:// www.salon.com/mwt/feature/2008/07/03/pregnant_man/index.html?source=newsletter.

23. Gar Swaffar, "Pregnant Man Separates from Wife," *Digital Journal*, April 20, 2012, http://www.digitaljournal.com/article/323324.

24. Ibid.

25. Guy Trebay, "He's Pregnant; You're Speechless," *New York Times*, June 22, 2008, http://www.nytimes.com/2008/06/22/fashion/22pregnant.html.

26. Beatie, "Labor of Love."

27. Goldberg and Thomson, "Barbara Walters Exclusive." See also "Pregnant US Man Hails 'Miracle,'" *BBC News*, April 4, 2008, http://news.bbc.co.uk/2/hi/americas/7330196 .stm.

28. Leading authors in the field include but are by no means limited to Simone de Beauvoir, Judith Butler, Tina Chanter, Anne Fausto-Sterling, Michel Foucault, Judith "Jack" Halberstam, bell hooks, Luce Irigaray, Julia Kristeva, Jacques Lacan, Audre Lorde, Gayle Rubin, and Eve Kosofsky Sedgwick.

29. Judith Butler, "Gender Regulations," in *Undoing Gender* (New York: Routledge, 2004), 42.

30. Luce Irigaray, "This Sex Which Is Not One," in *This Sex Which Is Not One*, trans. Catherine Porter and Carolyn Burke (Ithaca, NY: Cornell University Press, 1985), 23.

31. "Feminist theory gave us feminism, and gay theory helped give us gay rights. But unless we bring gender theory out of the ivory towers and put it to work in the streets, we may be witnessing the birth of a major philosophic movement that succeeds in politi- cizing practically everything but produces practically nothing in the way of organized, systemic social change. And that would be a pity." Riki Wilchins, *Queer Theory, Gender Theory: An Instant Primer* (Los Angeles: Alyson Books, 2004), 106.

"[Gender studies is] concerned with anything that disrupts, denaturalizes, rear- ticulates, and makes visible the normative linkages we generally assume to exist between the biological specificity of the sexually differentiated human body, the social roles and statuses that a particular form of body is expected to occupy, the subjectively experi- enced relationship between a gendered sense of self and social expectations of gender- role performance, and the cultural mechanisms that work to sustain or thwart specific configurations of gendered personhood." Susan Stryker, "(De)Subjugated Knowledges:

An Introduction to Transgender Studies," in *The Transgender Studies Reader*, ed. Susan Stryker and Stephen Whittle (New York: Routledge, 2006), 3.

32. Irigaray is one example of this line of reasoning. While she challenges the traditional symbolic conception of the "feminine," she also fails to offer an alternative conception, which lays her theory open to the criticism that she is simply reiterating the tradition itself. See Irigaray, "This Sex Which Is Not One." Janice Raymond is another, seating "the feminine" in a common history shared by women. See Janice G. Raymond, *The Transsexual Empire: The Making of the She-Male*. New York: Teachers College Press, 1994.

33. Simone de Beauvoir, *The Second Sex*, ed. and trans. H. M. Parshley (New York: Vintage Books, 1952), 267.

34. Ibid., 65.

35. Ibid., 726 (emphasis in original).

36. Michel Foucault, *The History of Sexuality*, vol. 1, *An Introduction*, trans. Robert Hurley (New York: Vintage Books, 1978), 26.

37. Ibid., 43.

38. Butler, *Gender Trouble*, 23.

39. See John Money, "Hermaphroditism, Gender and Precocity in Hyperadrenocorticism: Psychologic Findings," *Bulletin of the Johns Hopkins Hospital* 96, no. 6 (1955), 254. "The term *gender role* is used to signify all those things that a person says or does to disclose himself or herself as having the status of boy or man, girl or woman, respectively. It includes, but is not restricted to, sexuality in the sense of eroticism." Ibid., 254.

40. Heidegger, *Being and Time*, 19; H. 1 (emphasis in original).

41. Ibid., 261; H. 219.

42. Ibid., 33; H. 12.

43. The subject-object distinction in traditional thinking is the radical division between the kind of being that experiences and the kinds of things that are experienced, which relies on the presumption that the being doing the experiencing is some kind of identifiable "thing."

44. Heidegger is very fond of the word *immerschon*, which translates to "always already." The significance of the *immerschon* is that it highlights his split from the traditional subject-object distinction. Instead of trying to step back from whatever he is examining and trying to be objective about it, Heidegger is interested in its subjective meaningfulness, in the ways it is cared about or seen as important. Medically speaking, a "mother" is an entity that reproduces. This definition, however, says nothing at all about all the worlds of meaning that arise when we tell someone she is acting "just like her mother."

45. John Haugeland, "Heidegger on Being a Person," in *Dasein Disclosed: John Haugeland's Heidegger* (Cambridge, MA: Harvard University Press, 2013), 10.

46. Edmund Husserl, *Ideas Pertaining to a Pure Phenomenology and to a Phenomenological Philosophy: First Book, General Introduction to a Pure Phenomenology*, trans. F. Kersten (Boston: Kluwer Academic, 1983), 44 (emphasis in original).

47. René Descartes, *Meditations on First Philosophy*, trans. Donald A. Cress. (Indianapolis, IN: Hackett, 1993), 14.

48. Heidegger, *Being and Time*, 33; H. 12.

49. Ibid., 174–176; H. 134–137.

50. Ibid., 97; H. 68.

51. Ibid., 165–166; H. 128 (emphasis in original).

52. Ibid., 232; H. 188.

53. Ibid., 344; H. 298 (emphasis in original).

54. Ibid., 168; H. 130.

55. Ibid., 153; H. 117 (emphasis in original).

56. Heidegger, "What Is Metaphysics?" in *Martin Heidegger: Basic Writings*, ed. David Farrell Krell, trans. Albert Hofstadter (San Francisco: HarperCollins, 1993), 99–100.

57. Heidegger, *Being and Time*, 298; H. 254nxii.

58. For more on this topic, see Dorothy Leland, "Conflictual Culture and Authenticity: Deepening Heidegger's Account of the Social," in *Feminist Interpretations of Martin Heidegger*, ed. Nancy J. Holland and Patricia Huntington (University Park: Pennsylvania State University Press, 2001), 109–127.

59. Ibid., 119.

60. Kevin Aho, "Gender and Time: Revisiting the Question of Dasein's Neutrality," *Epoché* 12, no. 1 (2007): 149–150 (emphasis in original).

61. Heidegger, *Being and Time*, 165; H. 127.

62. Ibid., 181; H. 141.

63. Ibid., 291; H. 246.

64. Ibid., 37; H. 17.

65. A survey of the topics covered in Susan Stryker and Stephen Whittle, eds., *The Transgender Studies Reader* (New York: Routledge, 2006), which is representative of the main figures in transgender studies, yields insight into this focus on applied ethics and emancipatory discourse. The book begins with medical discourse, proceeds to questions of activism, provides histories of transgender individuals, addresses ethical issues, and closes with an examination of the intersections that obtain between gender, nationality, and race.

66. See also E. Das Janssen, "Queering Heidegger: An Applied Ontology," *Radical Philosophy Review* 16, no. 3 (2013): 747–762.

67. See Butler, *Gender Trouble*.

68. Judith Butler, "Preface," in *Bodies That Matter: On the Discursive Limits of "Sex"* (New York: Routledge, 1993), x.

69. This difficulty can be alleviated with Heidegger's model of Dasein.

70. Tina Chanter, "The Problematic Normative Assumptions of Heidegger's Ontology," in *Feminist Interpretations of Martin Heidegger*, ed. Nancy J. Holland and Patricia Huntington (University Park: Pennsylvania State University Press, 2001), 80; see also Jacques Derrida, "Geschlecht: Sexual Difference, Ontological Difference," in *Feminist Interpretations of Martin Heidegger*, ed. Nancy J. Holland and Patricia Huntington (University Park: Pennsylvania State University Press, 2001), 53–72 passim.

71. Leland, "Conflictual Culture and Authenticity," 113.

72. See chapter 3 for an account of Heidegger's account of *das Man* and its role.

73. Leland, "Conflictual Culture and Authenticity," 120.

74. Ibid., 125–126.

75. This book is no exception. It is necessarily perspectival, as it is written by a white trans man in middle age who enjoys the privilege of an education in philosophy. I urge wide reading about engagement with gender. It would be impossible to provide a full list of authors, but a few to start with are Kate Bornstein, Janet Mock, Julia Serano, Zachary Nataf, Susan Stryker, Gayle Salamon, and Gayle Rubin.

76. Rice University, "Is 'the Dress' White and Gold or Blue and Black? Visual Perception Expert Weighs In," *Science Daily*, March 2, 2015, http://www.sciencedaily.com/releases/2015/03/150302134235.htm.

77. See Leland, "Conflictual Culture and Authenticity."

78. E. Das Janssen, "Technologies of Gender: Heidegger, Foucault, and the Saving Power" (paper presented at the Fifty-Second Meeting of the Society for Phenomenology and Existential Philosophy, Eugene, OR, October 24–26, 2013).

79. Ibid.

CHAPTER 2

GENDER IN ITS HISTORICAL SITUATION

GENDER, AS IT is traditionally understood in the West, unravels and starts showing some interesting lacunae and confusions when examined closely. This chapter is about how these inconsistencies have led to the way gender is thought today. A broad survey of the history of the West reveals some significant transitions in the conception of "gender" since the Greeks, along with some revolutions in the way biological sex is conceived in myth, medicine, law, and religion. These revolutions, while interesting in themselves as historical phenomena, are even more interesting when examined in relation to one another in order to trace the variances in perception that have shaped the world. The phenomenon of gender is more mutable and more grounded in social and political concerns than is generally believed.

In gender theory, the nexus of debate is social construction theory, rather than biological essentialism, but the field of medicine still largely operates under an essentialist model. The historical account of how biological sex is assigned and conceived shows that science itself is a social construction, even given its essentialist leanings. Science is a project largely concerned with classificatory systems, and classificatory systems are not found in nature but are constructed by human thought. It is not that bodies are formed male or female or intersex in the womb and language reflects that. It is that bodies are formed, and then labels such as "male," "female," or "intersex" are assigned. Any knowledge of concrete facts about bodies is always already knowledge that is gained through the lens of social construction. Science operates within culture, which is to say it always exists within a web of belief, or set of presuppositions about reality, and that means that its conclusions are always already colored by the way questions are posed. Quite simply, comparisons cannot be made unless there are some preliminary criteria with which to make them.[1] A fundamental understanding of the phenomenon of gender is only possible if these preconceptions and their histories are examined and then evaluated in light of this context of intelligibility. The context of scientific principles and discoveries reveals as much about knowledge as the principles and discoveries themselves.

As most people understand sex and gender, they are closely related, and a body's sex will determine its gender. Maxine Sheets-Johnstone has pointed out that any performance of gender is performance by a body and that culture is always the culture of embodied beings.[2] Who individuals are and what possibilities are available to them have a great deal to do with what their bodies are like. A basketball player and a jockey have different possibilities for sport that are based in their animate form; an egg-bearing human and a sperm-bearing human have different possibilities for reproductive roles that are similarly based. Thus, it seems reasonable to suppose that cultural assumptions about bodies are based in actual facts of bodies themselves.

However, it does not follow from this that corporeality is more "true," or more foundational, than cultural conceptions of bodies. How can the sexed Being of bodies be understood except through language and cultural influence, which define "biological sex" and "gender"? How is it that there can be classifications, such as "male," "female," or "intersex," for the myriad forms in which bodies appear, except through discourse? And why is it that reproductive capacity is so widely regarded as such an important defining characteristic of human beings, anyhow? All animals reproduce; this is nothing special or particular to being human. There is no obvious reason to privilege reproduction over other kinds of difference or capacity. Since discourse is both the product and the generator of social construction, it is clear that the body is a phenomenon that is neither a mere product of discourse nor a raw, immutable fact. The only points of access there are for *understanding* embodiment are the culturally inscribed methods that articulate similarity and difference. Similarities and differences between bodies can be perceived only because there is already a method with which to examine them. So it certainly is correct that without embodiment, and the essential sexual difference that occurs in embodiment, the cultural constructions of gender and sexual difference as they are understood now would not be possible. But it is equally the case that without the cultural constructions of gender and sexual difference, the *intelligibility* of actual bodies, produced by nature in all their diversity, would not be possible. Males and females do not exist simply because nature makes human bodies of only two types. Nature produces a great variety of humans. Some are males and females primarily because of the labels applied to the variations that are encountered factually in bodies. Without the bodies, classification obviously would not occur. But without the classification, the bodies would not be something anyone could make sense of. "Biological sex" may seem to entail only observable facts about the body, but it is actually a classificatory system that presupposes that bodies will conform to certain definitive types and is thus gendered. "Gender" is pure social construction, but it is traditionally (though it does not have to be) predicated on biological type. That is, persons with the body defined by biology as female are expected to take on the feminine role in interaction with others; gender is expected to conform with biological sex.

This might seem at first to describe a vicious circle, and it would be if it addressed the question of logical implication or necessity, but it does not do this. Gender is a condition in which one always already finds oneself, so discussion of the issue of gender is a descriptive, historical project rather than an analysis of causes and effects.[3] The point of this inquiry is to find not the *causal* origin of gender but rather its factical, *existential* origin, its wellspring, the reason that at any time Dasein finds itself always already as having a "cultured body" and an "embodied culture" in its historical situation, something which shows itself pointedly in the phenomenon of Dasein's gender. The history of Dasein is precisely the history of this always already established and ongoing intertwining of body and culture in the site of gender. When children learn about the world, they do not first find "naked" physical things and then project "meanings" onto them; nor do they find free-floating Platonic meanings that are then matched up to things they experience. Rather, Dasein is always already *thrown* in the world, which is to say, it is always together with the world, interwoven with it. As it is correct that Dasein both encounters and constructs the world, it is also the case that Dasein finds itself in a body and constructs the intelligibility of that body in a structure of meaningfulness that can be described as a "virtuous circle."[4] So neither construction nor biological fact needs to be logically prior to the other in this analysis; rather, they can be understood as interdependent aspects of the phenomenon of gender. A great deal of literature and debate has been generated on the question of the priority of biological essence or social construction, which ultimately falls prey to the usual difficulties faced by Western dualist metaphysics, estranging two otherwise interdependent models of human sexual difference; the fact is, neither can make sense without the other. There is culture, and there is nature. Without nature, culture has no basis; without culture, nature cannot be articulated and understood. The two are not opposites, they are not mutually exclusive, and Dasein constructs its body, literally "incorporating experience into our very flesh."[5]

Why Examine the Historical Conception of the Body?

The popular conception that the sciences provide solid, indisputable fact that can be relied on as providing immutable truth is flawed; it ignores the fact that the scientific approach to questions is one approach among many and that the characteristics of the discipline shape its discoveries. The scientific project formulates questions in a particular way, and this formulation affects the outcome of the questioning process. In this sense, the scientific project discloses a "world," in the Heideggerian sense, in the way that the art world is spoken of as a "world." Scientific fact does not yield the capital-T "Truth"[6] of any thing but rather the way in which that thing is meaningful within an already existing world inhabited and lived by Dasein. The scientist sees what she expects to see, and Dasein is more likely to fit observations to the scripts that are operative in culture than it is to adopt any kind of radically objective viewpoint. Something is recognized as "true" when it fits together with a greater body of knowledge. Of course, there is no guarantee that there is any one context that is the correct one, particularly in the sciences, where multiple hypotheses may coexist. When scientists make determinations about observable data, what they are doing is interpreting those data in terms of an existing body of knowledge, which includes definitions and classificatory systems. For example, as long as the observable data regarding Pluto allowed it to fall into the category of being a planet, Pluto was regarded as a planet. When new data came forth about Pluto, it was demoted from planetary status to that of dwarf planet. All this relies not only on observations of Pluto but also on what a planet is understood to be and how the criteria of what constitutes a "planet" have been defined. Pluto has not changed; the understanding of Pluto has changed.

Something not unlike this has occurred more than once in the understanding of the human body and biological sex. Whereas medical theory has traditionally examined the "facts" of biology first, to determine what may or may not be corporally inherent about gender, the phenomenologist must approach the question from the opposite side. The question is not one of observing differences in bodies and then classifying those differences with names but rather of examining how preconceptions of gender have affected the science of human biology concerning sexual difference. How has the naming of things shaped what can be seen in them?

Since Plato, at least, Western thought has conceived of the human being as a combination of more or less discrete elements or substances, the physical and the nonphysical. The notion of the soul, which is the essence of the self, being trapped or contained in the body has been one of the paradigms that shape Western thinking. The relationship between the physical and the nonphysical has been the focus of much of the history of Western metaphysics and has influenced the way other disciplines have developed through the ages. Even those metaphysical theories that challenge this sort of dualism, such as Aristotle's, have been shaped by the way the mind-body relationship is conceived and the ways the questions have been asked. Traditionally, medicine, as the art or science of caring for the body, is concerned with the physical, whereas the care of the incorporeal soul falls under the aegis of religion and philosophy, and political theory and law concern themselves with both. But these mind-body distinctions are far from being radical; it is simply assumed that the incorporeal and the corporeal have some sort of interaction or relationship. They must, people tend to think, since they both contribute to the identity of human beings, and thus the expectation that certain kinds of bodies will produce matching kinds of souls, minds, or behaviors arises. As a result, the tradition has not only types of bodies, understood according to biological classifications, but also genders, which are the social roles, behaviors, and ways of thinking that are associated with types of bodies. Biological facts about bodies have traditionally created certain expectations regarding the genders that are associated with them, and ideas about gender have an effect on how bodies are understood and classified according to scientific observations.

This understanding of bodies, desires, and genders has developed along binary lines. Male and female are opposed to and more or less definitive of one another, as are masculine and feminine characteristics or behaviors. "Sexual orientations" are similarly defined as being along binary lines, and persons are described as being heterosexual, homosexual, bisexual, or asexual (in a binary system, the possibilities for "both" and "neither" may also be considered). In fact, there seem to be no necessary correlates between any of these three binaries at all. They describe *typical* sex, sexual orientations, and genders of human beings, but no factor seems to cause any other factor.

Some recent studies suggest that there may be a relationship between biology and gender or sexual orientation that is not predicated on the more obvious sex characteristics of bodies. This work is nascent and has produced no reliable results as of yet. What is suggested, at this early stage, is that there may be no single characteristic that influences gender or orientation but that there might possibly be a combination of influences.[7] I am less interested in biological causes of gender transgression or sexual orientation than in the ways that experience of gender and sexuality themselves drive and direct investigation, including the scientific. I am not arguing that medical discoveries ought to be disregarded, discounted, or discarded. But listening to medicine to the exclusion of philosophy, sociology, politics, and even personal stories told by individuals risks overlooking possibilities for how experience might be understood.

The difficulty with the traditional binary ways of thinking of the human self, biological sex, gender, and sexual orientation is that they create quite a muddle when these binaries are applied to real, living people who so inconveniently fall outside the limits of the various classifications. To sort out this mess, it is necessary to examine the ways in which these issues have been conceived throughout Western thought and how the binaries have played out under different conceptual models that carry their own presuppositions regarding the dualistic characteristics of the human being. These various binaries are distinct but related phenomena precisely, as Foucault would say, because the dominant discourse has so constructed them. The very language in which they are discussed is a language that relates these phenomena to one another. The sections that follow explore the ways in which Western thought has conceived of both the body and gender, and the results demonstrate that current conceptions of the various binary systems are not the only way they can be conceived but only the most recent way they are thought. This is not a strict historical analysis but rather something like Foucault's genealogical method that "de-realizes" the present to show how things have been different in the past and can be different in the future. This exercise can stimulate the imagining of other possibilities, ones that may not be obvious in ordinary, everyday concerns. Historically, the more tidy classifications established by science, the more exceptions to those classifications are discovered. The very persistence of these exceptions demonstrates that gender is not transhistorical. The contingency of classificatory systems reveals itself in exceptions and historical evolution. Human beings *will* just keep transgressing and exceeding whatever systems we may create.

The Greeks

Thomas Laqueur, in his *Making Sex: Body and Gender from the Greeks to Freud*, identifies two models of sexual difference used by Western medicine:

the one-sex model and the two-sex model. The former model holds that male and female humans are fundamentally the same, with corresponding anatomical parts, of which the female's are inverted versions of the male's. Female-bodied humans are seen not as different in kind from male-bodied humans but as imperfect versions of them, as can be seen in Aristotle, Augustine, and pretty much the rest of Western history until the late eighteenth century, when the latter model, the one with which most are familiar today, arose: that there are "fundamental differences between the male and female sexes, and thus between man and woman."[8] This was a radical change in the conception of human sexuality that also represents a radical change in the conception of human experience itself. Laqueur writes,

> [The] old model, in which men and women were arrayed according to their degree of metaphysical perfection, their vital heat, along an axis whose telos was male, gave way by the late eighteenth century to a new model of radical dimorphism, of biological divergence. An anatomy and physiology of incommensurability replaced a metaphysics of hierarchy in the representation of woman in relation to man.[9]

Whereas for most of Western history, human beings were classified hierarchically according to degree of greater or lesser perfection and according to an economy of heat and humors, with the male at the top, the model in the eighteenth century became one in which humans were classified according to bipolar types, each with its own kind of perfection, which provided a biological justification for the gender roles that society already demanded of its members. "Sex before the seventeenth century, in other words, was still a sociological and not an ontological category."[10] The upshot of Laqueur's research is that the medical understanding of biological sex is a product of previous cultural expectations. Neither the one-sex model nor the two-sex model is scientifically provable as the more "truthful" or accurate. Instead, the shift in cultural expectations is actually a shift in the context within which scientific observations are made and interpreted.

It is well known that Aristotle regarded the female as an imperfect version of the male.[11] He understood the bodies of males and females to operate under the same economy of fluid (the humors) and heat, and regarded the principal "imperfection" of the female to lie in the fact that she lacks the heat to become male. This was the predominant paradigm for Western medicine for many centuries, as can be seen see in Galen and others, although it was refined a great deal by the end of the medieval period. But a sufficiency or deficiency of heat is not an essential ontological distinction; it is, rather, a distinction between accidental qualities of human beings. This is significant because gender roles assigned to men and women were assigned on the basis of believed degrees of natural capacity or inclination for activity or passivity, not on the basis of their being different in kind. Masculine women and feminine men were part of the paradigm; they held places on a continuum of heat and fluid. Indeed, distinct nomenclature for female anatomy was not even developed until the Enlightenment. What was most important for most of Western history, then, was how closely one's body conformed to a single notion of perfection, not essential differences between the sexes. The distinction was thus metaphysical and political, not biological.

In both Plato and Aristotle, the observable biological differences between men and women are not nearly as important as their social roles. Aristophanes's descriptions of the origins of humans in Plato's *Symposium* makes it clear that male and female humans come from the same source,[12] and in the *Republic*, Plato introduces a very odd idea for the time when he discounts the necessity for different gender roles, except in the bearing of children, which is the only significant *biological* difference he recognizes between women and men.[13] Aristotle regards the family unit as constitutive of the *polis*, the proper structure of the family being rule by the husband and the goodness of women being essential to the goodness of the *polis* itself.[14] Furthermore, fatherhood, very much protected by the social system of the Greeks, is a sociological issue of gender, not an issue of biology. The issues of concern were power and legitimacy, and since the father of a child is more often a matter of doubt than the mother is, the social system was concerned with preserving his rights of control over the mother and child.[15] This social agenda, Laqueur argues, colored the way biological difference and similarity were understood in the ancient world; it was in turn constituted by ancient notions of masculinity and femininity, not by maleness and femaleness.

Concepts of femininity and masculinity in the ancient world included the notion that the masculine is active, spiritual, political, and intellectual, while the feminine is passive, material, homey, and irrational. Over and over again, these qualities are attributed to men and women, respectively. Aristotle noted that women do possess the rational part of the soul,[16] and also that "there is a special form of goodness for women."[17] The goodness of women is that which maintains the home, as a matter of political stability. This is a theme that can be found in the Greek understanding of the genders throughout the literature of the time: both men and women possess the capacity for virtue, but they achieve it in different ways. While there were specifically masculine and feminine virtues in the Greek world, there is also an interesting recurring theme in

Greek literature in which opposite-gender couples, usually kin, tend to manifest the same virtues and vices as their counterparts, but these are performed or exhibited in differently gendered fashion. Take the relationship of Odysseus and Penelope, for instance, as it is repeatedly contrasted to that of Agamemnon and Clytemnestra throughout the *Odyssey*.[18] The virtues of Odysseus, as Homer repeats again and again, are wiliness and loyalty. His cleverness gets him out of one scrape after another, and all his adventures are in pursuit of his goal: home and Penelope. But Penelope is no less wily and loyal. She outsmarts the suitors on more than one occasion, with the weaving and unweaving of Laertes's shroud and with the archery contest to which she subjects the suitors. When Odysseus finally returns home, she very cleverly tests him, guaranteeing by the rigor of the test not only that the man before her is indeed her husband but that he can be confident in her twenty years of faithfulness. Had it been too easy for Odysseus to convince Penelope that he was himself, he might have harbored doubts regarding her susceptibility to impostors. So, while Penelope and Odysseus both exhibit cleverness and loyalty, the ways in which they do so are very different. Odysseus travels, whereas Penelope remains at home, almost always in her own chamber. Odysseus always wins out in the end and thereby establishes dominance over his opponents. Penelope, on the other hand, wins out by feigning submission to her opponents, the suitors. At last, the virtuous couple achieves their mutual goal, the joyous reunion. While there is constant assistance from Athena, her role is a supporting one; she provides moral support, information, and aid, but there is no climactic deus ex machina in the *Odyssey* because none is needed. The protagonists' virtue carries them through to their reunion.

Agamemnon and Clytemnestra, on the other hand, are rather vicious. They do both share the virtue of convincing leadership, as evidenced by Agamemnon's competence in the Trojan War and Clytemnestra's ruling of Mycenae, but they are also both faithless and both commit the heinous crime of spilling family blood. Agamemnon is faithless toward Achilles when he takes Briseis, a war prize, from the hero. Clytemnestra, for her part, takes a lover during Agamemnon's extended absence at the war. The vicious acts that seal their fates, however, are Agamemnon's sacrifice of Iphigenia and Clytemnestra's murder of Agamemnon in revenge. Agamemnon and Clytemnestra both come to a bad end, and their actions threaten the entire House of Atreus. Agamemnon's crime in sacrificing his daughter, while not exactly illegal, is nevertheless a betrayal of trust that is bad enough, but Clytemnestra's offense is twofold: not only does she commit the horrific act of kin-murder, but she also oversteps the bounds of what behaviors are acceptable for women in the

Greek culture, both by entering the public sphere as ruler and by undertaking the revenge-murder of Agamemnon. As a consequence, she sets in motion a cycle of revenge-killings demanded first by the Furies and then by Apollo, as told in the *Oresteia*, which has the potential to wipe out the entire royal family of Mycenae. Only Athena's timely arrival and institution of a trial by jury saves the House of Atreus from utter ruin. In this case, virtue does not win the day, and deus ex machina is necessary to maintain the social order.

The juxtaposition of these two couples tells a story of more than mere adventure; it shows how virtues are properly or improperly performed by men and women according to the Greek standards. Furthermore, crossing gender lines is almost always negative when it is a man whose behavior is conceived as feminine, but it is frequently positive when it is a woman whose behavior is conceived as masculine. Herodotus notes with admiration a certain Sesostris, an Egyptian king, who honored the enemies he defeated in honorable battle with pillars that lauded their bravery, but for those who abdicated, Sesostris erected pillars that bore an image of a vagina.[19] Even the gods are subject to expectations regarding gender. Dionysus is described as possessing feminine qualities, "long yellow curls smelling of perfumes, with flushed cheeks and the spells of Aphrodite in his eyes. His days and nights he spends with women and girls, dangling before them the joys of initiation into his mysteries."[20] This gender transgression of Dionysus's presents a danger to the ordered, rational world of Greek men precisely because he personifies feminine qualities, and it results in the destruction of the king of Thebes himself, who, besides being a man, is a representative of the social order. The king, and symbolically the social order, too, is destroyed, ripped limb from limb by women who have abandoned reason on their descent into mania; the king's own mother displays his head in triumph.

Women who take on the qualities of men, on the other hand, are regarded as both dangerous and admirable in the ancient world. Two women in Herodotus's *The History* are particularly impressive: Queen Tomyris of the Massagetae, who successfully leads her army against Cyrus, defeating him and defiling his corpse,[21] and Artemisia, an adviser of Xerxes who took her deceased husband's place in war, serving "out of pure spirit and manliness, with no compulsion on her to do so."[22] In the Battle of Salamis, the Athenians offered a prize of ten thousand drachmas for her capture. She outsmarted the Greeks by ramming one of the Persian ships, making the Greeks think hers was one of their own ships, and thus escaped. Xerxes, upon hearing this, observed, "My men have become women, and my women men."[23] In Greek literature, there is a wealth of women who distinguish themselves with displays of power. There is Helen, of course, whose abandonment of her husband and home precipitates the Trojan War. And there is also Antigone, who, by the act of burying her brother, steps out of the realm of the household and family and into the political sphere. These examples illustrate the way the metaphysical hierarchy that designates the male and masculine as the higher order of being is played out in the exemplification of gender in the arts and reportage, which is carried over to the expectations placed on women and men within the social sphere. They also illustrate that gender roles were a political matter more than biological determination—women and men did (and do) cross the gender divide, with results that vary but almost always favor the masculine.

The Christian World

With the advent of Christianity arrived a shift in values that affected the genders quite drastically. For the most part, the scientific paradigms of the ancients endured throughout the medieval period, but the social expectations of men and women effected a revolution in how gender was thought. The period still operated on the one-sex model, but the predominant paradigm was no longer an economy of heat and fluid but one of the will, thanks to Saint Augustine and other church fathers. The Christian values passivity in the face of God's will, emphasizes human corporeality as contrasted with an incorporeal God, and favors mystical, religious faith over reason. Further, in restricting the power of fathers by forbidding infanticide, promoting virginity and chastity, and reorganizing the religious life, Christianity radically restructured the cultural denotation of gender along with the rest of the social order. It came to pass that many characteristics that had been considered effeminate in the ancient paradigm become the ideal in the Christian era.[24] The framework is the same; the values have been reorganized. Augustine could write the tearful *Confessions* and, because of his submission to God, be regarded as that much more admirable than a Pagan man who epitomized the warrior values of the Greeks and Romans. This shift in Western thought is crucial, because it demonstrates that gender roles must be determined by cultural values rather than by biological necessity. The one-sex model survived several centuries before it was presented with any serious challenge, but the two-gender model was transformed into a one-gender model. That is, the virtues of men and women are not different virtues; nor are they properly manifested in different ways, as they were in the Greek world. As Clement of Alexandria says, "the virtue of man and woman is the same,"[25] and their only real distinction is in marriage. Augustine attributes to women "an equal capacity for rational intelligence" even while he insists that women must remain subordinate to men.[26] Of course, in the medieval period, men were still regarded as more perfect than women, and now the hierarchy had the advantage of being ordained by God. Yet women *did* make it into the higher echelons of social approbation. There were female martyrs and saints, such as Thecla, Vibia Perpetua, and Blandina, who apparently had the approbation of God himself, contradicting the absolute inferiority of women.[27] Such exemplary models of Christian values who were also female had to be accounted for. This brings up an interesting feature of gender in the Christian era: its very malleability. All the attacks on women in the medieval period—and they were many—notwithstanding, there were women who were admired and admitted to the company of saints. Instead of granting that some women might be superior to some men, however, masculinity was attributed to these women. Jerome said of the woman who served Christ faithfully, "then she will cease to be a woman and will be called man."[28] Indeed, many women did just this in corporeal life as well. There are over thirty saints who are documented as female-to-male cross-dressers in the medieval period, and many of them lived permanently as men.[29] All this indicates that gender assignment in the West prior to the advent of the Enlightenment (and for quite some time afterward) was more a matter of social prescription than personal type or inclination. While the prescriptions were rather rigid and unsuited to change, individuals could pass from one category to the other. An individual's gender could be re-prescribed by papal fiat more easily than the concept of woman could be expanded to include strong figures! The classificatory system that governed gender was actually one that had little to do with biological type, except insofar as biological type dictated reproductive capacity and thus familial and social role. In cases where reproduction was not an issue, gender boundaries could be crossed quite legitimately, even with the church's blessing.

It would be a grave error to underemphasize the truly nasty misogyny of the medieval period; the condemnations of women and the feminine in literature are well known. But this common misogyny is not a one-dimensional attitude. The image of Mary as a feminine aspect of the divine gained popularity as the medieval period waxed. The existence of actual strong women and the portrayal of such women in literature is juxtaposed with a dominant discourse that characterized women as weak, passive, irrational, emotional, lustful, and disorderly.[30] For the most part, this discourse was proliferated by male writers of the period. Female writers "paid surprisingly little attention to their supposed incapacity."[31] This juxtaposition suggests a complex system of symbolism at work rather than a literal characterization of particular human beings. And in this symbolic system, genders and even physical sexual characteristics were not conceived of as mutually exclusive but rather as mixtures in actual bodies. Not only did the virtues of men and women such as asceticism, piety, and devotion to Christ overlap,[32] but the body too was seen as incorporating both male and female elements.

> To say this is not to deny that men were seen as superior in rationality and strength. Clearly they were. But existing, particular human beings were understood as having both womanly and virile characteristics. Moreover, we must never forget the emphasis on reversal that lay at the heart of the Christian tradition. According to Christ and to Paul, the first shall be last and the meek shall inherit the earth.[33]

The images of strong women in art and culture are consistent with the theme of reversal that is central to Christian thinking. No less are the stories of those women who transgressed gender boundaries in literature and life consistent with this theme, since they literally manifested the masculine qualities of their female bodies and characters.

What all this shows is that in the medieval period, gender, and the feminine gender in particular, was regarded as something that was subject to such reversal. The medieval experience of gender is malleable and alterable, and might even arise as a consequence of the will to serve God faithfully, rather than of biological fact or political obligation. It must be a matter of will, since the masculinity of the female saints is due to their holiness, and holiness always involves the choice to turn to God. Whereas in the Greek world gender reversals upset the order of things, in the Christian world gender reversals in which women took on virile qualities confirmed the order of things, and the women who underwent such reversals were admired and understood to be bettering themselves within an ontological hierarchy and moving closer to God. The same cannot be said of cross-dressing males. There are no accounts of male saints who wore women's clothing, and while male cross-dressing was tolerated in the theater, it was done only within a very narrow context, where there was no question of the actor passing as the opposite gender in daily life. A man who donned the garb of a woman outside the theater was prosecuted as a criminal, as in the case of John Rykener, a male cross-dressing prostitute.[34] There is no tradition of male-to-female cross-dressing in literary or hagiographical themes. The historical record, too, is strikingly silent on the subject. The Rykener case is notable precisely because it appears to be the only available English legal-process document that deals with homosexual acts in the late medieval period, and later catalogers of such documents obscured its existence.[35] It would seem that reversals in which men became more feminine were so "libidinous and unspeakable"[36] as to be also unthinkable. Anatomical observations took place within a culture in which there were high political stakes for gender conformity. The one-sex model, even after becoming something more like a one-gender model, was formed within a web of belief that retained the notion that women's inherent—and surmountable—imperfections, and not difference in kind, were the source of their alterity and a justification for a specific social role. In noncorporeal matters, then, a woman could be a man's equal; in corporeal matters, she was to be subordinate. This poses a sharp contrast to the Greek understanding of the feminine as, by definition, imperfect.

The Enlightenment and Today

In the Enlightenment, new scientific methods and values emerged. No longer was it acceptable to rely on ancient commentary for scientific data. "Rules and formulas, those mechanical aids to the rational use, or rather misuse, of [the scientist's] natural gifts, are the shackles of a permanent immaturity."[37] Actual observation became the standard, and difference, rather than similarity, became the focus of classification. Instead of seeing sex as a continuum of greater and lesser perfections, scientists began to classify male and female anatomy differently. All the old names for the generative organs were retained by the male body, and the organs of the female body were named anew. For example, the organ that had been called "female penis" was christened "vagina," which reveals much about how the female reproductive organs were understood. ("Vagina" is the Latin for "sheath," an object whose meaning and purpose are inextricably tied to what fits inside it.) This shift is only one aspect of a larger movement in which the ancient and medieval notion of the body as microcosm of the natural order (wherein similarity and frequently even metaphor, along with *telos*, were the primary criteria for classification) was replaced by the passion for difference and distinction observable in the system of Carl Linnaeus, which is still used today, with some modification. The criteria for classification became the ways in which organisms differed, not their similarities, and specificity became the goal of classification, at least within the scientific world. Since the differences between male and female humans seemed to be so easily observable, it is hardly surprising that science took the attitude of distinction toward them and began to emphasize difference rather than similarity.[38] Thus was the two-sex model of human sexuality born. Such a classificatory system, it must be noted, is inherently exclusionary; it describes the typical by means of excluding the atypical. Even when the ease of observability was later challenged with the discovery of hormones and chromosomes, the presupposition that there *are* two distinct sexes has endured for decades, and the gender differences already in place seemed to be justified by these differences—women were no longer regarded as passive because they were undeveloped men, or because their humors were cooler, but because of their different biology. And yet the old presupposition that human sex is binary continued to thrive. The question was, and continues to be: What are the differences between the sexes? It is not: What is meant by "sexes"?[39]

Politically, the climate of the eighteenth century was one of revolution. Old assumptions regarding nobility and commoners, rich and poor, and women and men were, sometimes literally, on the chopping block. It is in the Enlightenment that individual rights came to the forefront of political thinking, and the combination of science's development as a system of classification based on difference and the contemporary political climate in which the liberty and equality of citizens under the law made for some complex developments in the conceptions of body and gender. Certainly, the ways that sex and gender began to be discussed were highly influenced by Enlightenment conceptions of personhood and citizenship. They were also influenced by colonialist tendencies that actively policed any deviation from a narrow ideal, forcing it into the mold demanded by "civilization," "humanism," and "propriety." A result of this is that a great deal of the discourse concerning sex and gender from the Enlightenment and after is legislative in nature. Deviation from expected comportments and orientations raises questions of how laws will be drafted to accommodate citizens' needs.

Whereas the Greek model of the body and gender was seated in the good of the *polis* and the medieval model in the presumed will of God, the Enlightenment model of two sexes and two natural genders came about as a result of the tension between the scientific model of two distinct sexes and the political ideal of humanism, which places supreme value on the human individual. Women in this period began to enjoy more rights as individuals within society, even while the differences between men and women were increasingly emphasized. Some thinkers, such as Mary Wollstonecraft and John Stuart Mill, even began to question the politically subordinate status of women and gave birth to the feminist movement, which was to rely heavily on the idea of essential differences between the sexes until the late twentieth century.[40] The first and second waves of the feminist movement challenged the notion that the feminine is inferior but did not question the basic, binary, exclusionary structure of the system that defines the feminine as that which is not masculine.

The upshot of all this is that today the relationship of the body to gender is quite a muddle, and the question of gender is becoming more and more urgent in the political and social spheres. There is the male-female binary, and there is the masculine-feminine binary, and they intersect in many different ways.

Thanks to the discovery of chromosomes and hormones, scientists and philosophers know a great deal more about biological sex than ever before. This has
precipitated a whole set of questions about how to classify sex, especially since
the characteristics according to which they are classified are no longer as easily
observable as they were once presumed to be. Just to make things really interesting, the persistence of atypical bodies resists attempts to clarify what is meant by
male and female. The more that is learned, the less existing categories suffice to
describe or accommodate observations. It is becoming more difficult to assign
one sex or the other to many newborns, since knowing more about sex differences is precisely what allows the identification of exceptions to the tidy classifications that used to seem so simple. There are now at least fifteen recognized
types of intersex condition, and it is estimated that about one in one hundred
births are of bodies that do not fulfill the "standard" criteria used to classify a
body as either female or male, and one or two in every thousand receive surgery
to bring bodies into conformity with the classificatory systems that are established by scientific and cultural tradition.[41] To give an example that puts these
statistics in perspective, they would mean that if the average were to hold, out of
8 million residents of New York City alone, eighty thousand would not fit all the
criteria for classification as either male or female. In statistical terms, 1 percent
is not all that much. But in terms of human lives lived, this is a rather significant
number of people. Of course, these statistics are mere estimates, and there are
various reasons for this. The medical records of some intersex persons are sealed
by the courts, which prevents their inclusion in both statistical measurements
and also follow-up observation.[42] In many other cases, intersex conditions are
simply not readily observable. Take XX males, for instance. These are male-
bodied individuals, born with penises that function for sexual purposes, who
experience typical bodily changes at puberty and have no reason to suppose
they might be intersex. But they possess XX chromosomes, and they typically
discover their condition only when they are having trouble conceiving and have
a full physical work-up. This means that the only XX males being counted are
those who desire to become parents and who have access to the kind of health
care that allows for the very expensive testing required to identify their chromo-
somal anomaly, which is a very small percentage of male-bodied persons overall. The truth is, nobody knows how many bodies are classifiable as intersex. As
a general rule, bodies are not tested for consistent classifiability as one sex or the
other, but rather sex is assumed, based on genital shape.

A related issue is the existence of the gender transgressive individual. In
1925, Magnus Hirschfeld published *Transvestites: The Erotic Drive to Cross-
Dress*, which was the first in-depth study of a phenomenon that has been ob-

served throughout history: the drive some people have to wear the clothing assigned to the opposite sex or gender from the one to which they are expected to conform. Hirschfeld regarded "the essence of clothing [to be] a symbol, an unconscious projection of the soul"[43] and cross-dressing to be an outward manifestation of a kind of intermediary soul that is neither fully male nor fully female. He describes one case thus:

> Miss T. had always felt dissatisfied with her women's clothes, because they prevented her from living in agreement with her inner tendency. In women's clothing she appeared to the public as worthy of mocking, especially by the street youth. . . . Whereas her external appearance used to attract attention and incite public annoyance to a certain degree, [now that she wears men's clothing] this is no longer the case. Consequently, her mood, which used to be depressed, has lifted. Her wish to maintain this condition is easy for anyone to understand.[44]

Gender expression is not simply about clothing, although clothing is frequently one very visible aspect of such transgression. It is, rather, about a way of being in the world that is in agreement or disagreement with some "inner tendency." Sometimes something causes a person to experience discomfort with their assigned gender role, and this discomfort is frequently strong enough to interfere with the individual's being able to function and thrive as a member of their community. Transvestism is one such phenomenon, but it is by no means the only one. Transsexuality, transgender, and genderqueer[45] are all phenomena that involve the transgression or outright rejection of gender binaries and thus pose a serious challenge to the binaries themselves. New terms and concepts spring up all the time. In spite of the tidy classifications that medicine and jurisprudence use to try to simplify us away, people who are gender transgressive persist. This persistence challenges the traditional vocabulary and conceptual models used to conceive of persons. Those who do not fit existing classificatory systems in the expected ways may be silenced by the very lack of terminology with which experience can be expressed, and sometimes they assert a way of Being by creating new terminology. As Harry Benjamin, who continued Hirschfeld's work, puts it,

> Our sexuality has to be without fault. It must function in strict conformity with customs and laws, no matter how illogical they may be and to how much hypocrisy they may give rise.
>
> Any interference with the sacrosanct stability of our sex is one of the great tabus [sic] of our time. Therefore, its violation is strongly resented with emotions likely to run high, even among doctors.[46]

Yet such people *do persist* and are beginning to develop the vocabulary and conceptual models that describe these experiences and "inner tendencies." Questions are coming up that would have been nonsensical a mere sixty years ago, such as "Can and should bodies be altered in order to make people more comfortably fit the gender binary?" and "Ought legal institutions be altered to account for those citizens whose bodies do not fit the sex and gender binaries recognized by those institutions?" In twenty-first century America, medical fields still operate, for the most part, under the two-sex model of human biology, but social and legal institutions have to reckon with some very intriguing challenges to the two-gender model. Uncloseted transgender children are entering school, as young as kindergarten-age.[47] These children raise questions that are not easily answered or avoided, and Western culture is faced with examining just what it means to be a boy or girl, man or woman.

Aside from the fact that it is clear that there is no known biological determinant of gendered experience or behavior, and that the notion of gender being essentially linked to biology has come under serious scrutiny, pressing issues of sexual orientation demand attention. It is difficult, although not impossible, to articulate issues of sexual orientation independently of biological sex and gender. Benjamin's work on transsexuality assumes that homosexuality is "a sex problem,"[48] and that the desirable result of sex reassignment surgery is a heterosexual patient, even while he also points out that the differences between male and female bodies are differences of degree with regard to a continuum, rather than differences of kind.[49] The requirements are no longer so rigid, but requirements that a transsexual patient submit to stringent regulations regarding competence and ability to live in the "target gender" still persist. A rhinoplasty can be had for the asking and paying of the bill; not so a vaginoplasty. Transsexuality is pathologized, yet transsexual people are also frequently denied the means of treatment afforded other illnesses or disorders, such as insurance coverage.

Even the accuracy of the scientific understanding of bodies has come into question, since it is clear that neither the one-sex nor the two-sex model is provable scientifically, because each is conceived within the context of the web of belief in which it operates. Each model is true, in the sense that each model works to express and describe differences and similarities, but there is no perspective from which the absolute truth of either model can be declared. There is no God's-eye view of the truth. Truths of observation are dependent on the phenomenal world in which they are posited. What both models have in common, however, is the fact that biologists have consistently asked, "What are the differences?" and not *"Are* there differences?" The problem with the former question is that, prior to investigation, presupposition shapes the way answers can appear by already assuming the existence of differences, whereas the latter asks whether an answer to the former exists in the first place. This is important: differences exist, to be sure, but a phenomenological approach allows them to emerge, rather than sorting reality into a system that is assumed prior to observation.

In addition to this, political systems that demand equal treatment of and protection for citizens, regardless of race, religion, disability, sex, gender, or orientation, must be satisfied. In the current era, the political commitment to the rights of citizens, a driving discourse, is a force that demands to be reckoned with. As a consequence, Western nations are faced with foundational egalitarian issues in the form of intersex activism, transsexuality, transgender rights, and marriage equality. On one hand, the questions raised by the capacity to alter bodies to suit a gendered model of biological sex, in the cases of both intersex infants and of transsexual persons, shake the very foundations of how both the body and social expectations are conceived. (For instance, should the Affordable Care Act require insurance companies to cover hormone treatment for transsexual clients?) On the other hand, the questions of marriage equality and transgender rights are, at heart, the question of whether legal institutions should be altered to suit bodies as they do already exist. (For instance, should there be more categories than "male" and "female" on legal identification documents?) There have always been individuals who did not fit the expectations of their gender roles, either because their biology has not fallen within the range of what is considered "normal" or because their gendered behavior has transgressed social expectations, but for the first time in history there is a demand that medicine and the law do more than simply pathologize, canonize, or outlaw such individuals and behaviors. Medicine now has the capacity to change the bodies of individuals in order to bring them into conformity with the biological sex associated with the gender as which they identify, and, no less importantly, political and bureaucratic mechanisms exist that allow some to demand that legal institutions (such as marriage) be altered in order to include those individuals whose exclusion is currently based on such physical criteria as biological sex. (As the recent Supreme Court ruling confirms, there is no longer any contract in the United States federal legal system for which the legal or biological sex of the signatories is a relevant criterion for validity. The contradiction that forbade same-sex marriage while also precluding discrimination with regard to protection of rights based in citizens' biological sex or gender has been resolved. At the time of this writing, marriage equality is still very much an historical event in process; the Supreme Court has ruled bans on marriage equality unconstitutional, and disputing legislative actions are in the process of being drafted and filed.) There is a twofold demand here: that bodies change if individuals need them to and that gender expectations change as society needs them to. What they will change into has yet to be seen, but it is clear that Western culture is facing some serious challenges to traditional models of "biological sex" and "gender."

Today's revolutionary climate can be seen in how gendering occurs, in the visibility of gender issues in the social sphere: LGBT issues such as marriage equality are largely gender issues, even when they are characterized as being about sexuality. Caitlyn Jenner's life is subject to public scrutiny, a man has gone public about giving birth, a transgender teen has committed suicide and posted the note on social media, and transgender children are profiled on 20/20. The idea that is growing today is that nobody can tell what gender a person is except that person. That is what words like "transgender" and "transsexual" mean, at heart—that some make the claim that their gender and their biological type do not match up in the ways that society has come to expect; a crossing is occurring. But has this always been the case? Certainly, at all points in history there have been those who fit the social roles assigned to them less easily than others, but this did not create the shift apparent today. The transition from one conception of gender to another is key to how gender is understood for everyone, not only intersex, transgender, and transsexual individuals. Whereas today gender is seen as *descriptive* of types of people, it has in the past been understood to be *prescriptive* of social status, standing, and role. Much of the difficulty trans people face is due to resistance to this change in how gender is thought but also in the notion of personal rights. By all means, people who have not fit their assigned gender role have always existed. What is new is the demand for political recognition and legitimacy that has not been previously codified in Western history. The shift in emphasis from the smooth operation of the social order to the concept of individual rights has made this possible. One key point of the current Western understanding of rights is that *the atypical have rights too.* This notion has been key to all the aspects of the grand civil rights movement that compose the history of the United States, including the women's movement, the black civil rights movement, and the disability rights movement. Challenges to the notions that the typical citizen is white, male, and able-bodied and the current challenge of assignable gender all stem from the same idea: all persons have rights, including the right to differ from whatever norm is set up by history and heritage.

To summarize, then, in the Greek world bodies were understood as falling on various gradations of a continuum measured according to heat and fluid, but genders were strictly delineated because what was at stake was the maintenance of the *polis* and the patriarchal household as a foundational unit of the *polis*. The medieval understanding of the body was a refined version of the Greek one-sex model, but there was a shift from a two-gender model to a one-gender model, with gender being as much a matter of personal will and proximity to divine perfection as a political issue. The Enlightenment saw another shift, this time a dual one, to a two-sex and a two-gender model, in which new understandings of both sex and gender arose out of the tension that obtained between scientific observation and a new concern with political justice to the individual. Today offers yet another shift, in a challenge to the very binary characters of sex and of gender, even while providing less space for the existence of transgressive individuals in the social milieu than was afforded in the past. Add to this technologies that allow for sexual reassignment, technologies that allow atypical individuals to make contact with one another and build identities on their very atypicality, and the current debate regarding the accommodation of the differences of atypical individuals, guaranteeing or denying them political equality, and there is a whole lot going on. The persistence and visibility of atypical individuals, combined with the shifts in the conception of gender undergone throughout Western history, demonstrate that any understanding of gender and biological sex are contingent; there are other possibilities for how their relationship to one another can be understood. There are, in short, other possibilities for how human Being itself can be understood. It's a muddle, all right. And it is a muddle that must be addressed for the sake of both scientific accuracy and justice.

NOTES

1. Michel Foucault, *The Order of Things: An Archaeology of the Human Sciences* (New York: Random House, 1970), xx.

2. Maxine Sheets-Johnstone, *The Roots of Power: Animate Form and Gendered Bodies* (Chicago: Open Court, 1994), 62, 68–69, 70–71.

3. See Heidegger, *Being and Time*, 363; H. 315.

4. Ibid., 194–195; H. 152–153.

5. Fausto-Sterling, *Sexing the Body*, 20.

6. Heidegger, *Being and Time*, 93; H. 64–65; Martin Heidegger, "The Origin of the Work of Art," in *Martin Heidegger: Basic Writings*, ed. David Farrell Krell, trans. Albert Hofstadter (San Francisco: HarperCollins, 1993), 145.

7. Such studies include investigations into differences in brain structure, the structure of the hypothalamus, neuroendocrine structures, and genetic trends linked to the X chromosome. See Simon LeVay, "A Difference in Hypothalamic Structure between Heterosexual and Homosexual Men," *Science* 253 (1991): 1034–1037; J. M. Bailey and

R. C. Pillard, "A Genetic Study of Male Sexual Orientation," *Archives of General Psychiatry* 48, no. 12 (1991): 1089–1095.

8. Thomas Laqueur, *Making Sex: Body and Gender from the Greeks to Freud* (Cambridge, MA: Harvard University Press, 1990), 5. This is a conceptual history, describing general paradigm, and not an accounting of specific beliefs, which were naturally much more varied than presented here.

9. Ibid., 5–6.

10. Ibid., 8.

11. Aristotle, *The Complete Works of Aristotle*, ed. and trans. Jonathan Barnes, vol. 1, *Generation of Animals* (Princeton, NJ: Princeton University Press, 1984). "The deficient development of her body compared with a man's is obvious." 727a25. "Now a boy is like a woman in form, and the woman is as it were an impotent male, for it is through a certain incapacity that the female is female, being incapable of concocting the nutriment in its last stage into semen . . . owing to the coldness of her nature." 728a16–21. "We must look upon the female character as being a sort of natural deficiency." 775a14–15. "For the female is, as it were, a mutilated male, and the menstrual fluids are semen, only not pure; for there is only one thing they have not in them, the principle of soul." 737a27–29. He says of generation, "While the body is from the female, it is the soul that is from the male, for the soul is the substance of a particular body." 738b25–26. He says of monstrosities, "The first departure [from the ideal type] is that the offspring should become female instead of male; this, however, is a natural necessity." 767b8–9.

12. Plato, *Symposium*, trans. Michael Joyce, in *The Collected Dialogues of Plato*, ed. Edith Hamilton and Huntington Cairns (Princeton, NJ: Princeton University Press, 1938), 189d–193d.

13. Plato, *Republic*, trans. Paul Shorey, in *The Collected Dialogues of Plato*, ed. Edith Hamilton and Huntington Cairns (Princeton, NJ: Princeton University Press, 1938), 451d–457c.

14. Aristotle, *Politics*, ed. and trans. Ernest Barker (New York: Oxford University Press, 1946), xv, 1260b.

15. Laqueur, *Making Sex*, 57. Of course, such control would be unnecessary in Plato's City of Words, since parenthood was itself conceived of as radically different than it actually was in the Greek world.

16. Aristotle, *Politics*, vii, 1259b20–1260a19.

17. Ibid., xi, 1260a19–1260b18.

18. John Rees Moore, "Voyaging with Odysseus: The Wile and Resilience of Virtue," *Humanitas* 8, no. 1 (2000): 103–127.

19. Herodotus, *The History*, trans. David Grene (Chicago: University of Chicago Press, 1987), 2.102.

20. Euripides, *The Bacchae*, trans. David Grene and Richmond Lattimore (Chicago: University of Chicago Press, 1959), 235–238.

21. Herodotus, *The History*, 1.205–1.216.

22. Ibid., 7.99.

23. Ibid., 8.88. See also 8.68, 8.87, 8.101–8.103.

24. See Friedrich Nietzsche, *Beyond Good and Evil*, trans. Walter Kaufmann (New York: Vintage Books, 1966), 260; and Friedrich Nietzsche, *On The Genealogy of Morals*, trans. Carol Diethe (Cambridge: Cambridge University Press, 1994), 18–27.

25. Clement of Alexandria, "Paedagogus," in *The Ante-Nicene Fathers: Translations of the Writings of the Fathers Down to A.D. 325*, ed. Alexander Roberts and James Donaldson (Peabody, MA: Hendrickson, 1994), 212.

26. Augustine, *Confessions*, trans. Henry Chadwick (Oxford: Oxford University Press, 1991), XIII.xxxii (47).

27. Kim Power, *Veiled Desire: Augustine on Women* (New York: Continuum, 1996), 57.

28. Jerome, "Commentarius in Epistolam ad Ephesios," in *Patrologica Latina*, ed. J. P. Minge, vol. 26 (Paris: Garnier, 1884), 3.5.

29. See Valerie R. Hotchkiss, appendix to *Clothes Make the Man: Female Cross Dressing in Medieval Europe* (New York: Garland, 1996).

30. Carolyn Walker Bynum, "'. . . And Woman His Humanity': Female Imagery in the Religious Writing of the Later Middle Ages," in *Fragmentation and Redemption: Essays on Gender and the Human Body in Medieval Religion* (New York: Zone Books, 1991), 151.

31. Ibid., 155.

32. Ibid., 154.

33. Caroline Walker Bynum, "The Body of Christ in the Later Middle Ages: A Reply to Leo Steinberg," *Fragmentation and Redemption: Essays on Gender and the Human Body in Medieval Religion* (New York: Zone Books, 1991), 108–109.

34. See Paul Halsall, "The Questioning of John Rykener, a Male Cross-Dressing Prostitute, 1395," Fordham University, May 1998, http://www.fordham.edu/halsall/source/1395rykener.html.

35. Ibid.

36. Ibid.

37. Immanuel Kant, "An Answer to the Question, What Is Enlightenment?" in *Perpetual Peace and Other Essays on Politics, History, and Morals*, trans. Ted Humphrey (Indianapolis, IN: Hackett, 1983), 41.

38. Laqueur, *Making Sex*, 10.

39. Ibid., 152.

40. See Mary Wollstonecraft, *A Vindication of the Rights of Women*, ed. Carol H. Poston (New York: W. W. Norton, 1987); and John Stuart Mill, "The Subjection of Women," in *The Basic Writings of John Stuart Mill*, ed. Dale E. Miller (New York: Modern Library, 2002), 123–232.

41. Intersex Society of North America, "How Common Is Intersex?" The types of intersex conditions listed are not XX and not XY, Klinefelter syndrome, androgen insensitivity syndrome, partial androgen insensitivity syndrome, classical congenital adrenal hyperplasia, late onset adrenal hyperplasia, vaginal agenesis, ovotestes, idiopathic, iatrogenic, 5-alpha reductase deficiency, mixed gonadal dysgenesis, complete gonadal dysgenesis, hypospadias in perineum or along penile shaft, and hypospadias between corona and tip of glans penis.

42. See Wilchins, *Queer Theory, Gender Theory*.

43. Magnus Hirschfeld, *Transvestites: The Erotic Drive to Cross-Dress*, trans. Michael A. Lombardi-Nash (Buffalo, NY: Prometheus Books, 1991), 214.

44. Ibid., 153.

45. "Genderqueer" means, literally, "queering" gender, deliberately disrupting and derealizing gender norms.

46. Harry Benjamin, *The Transsexual Phenomenon* (New York: Julian Press, 1966), 10.

47. Ilene Lelchuck, "When Is It OK for Boys to Be Girls, and Girls to Be Boys?" *San Francisco Chronicle*, August 27, 2006, http://www.sfgate.com/cgi-bin/article.cgi?file=/c/a/2006/08/27/MNGL2KQ8H41.DTL.

48. Benjamin, *The Transsexual Phenomenon*, 26, 28.

49. Ibid., 28, 168.

CHAPTER 3

HEIDEGGER TROUBLE: GENDERED DASEIN AND EMBODIMENT

One common criticism of Heidegger's fundamental ontology is its failure to provide a robust account of Dasein's embodiment.[1] While he does give a robust critique of Descartes's *res extensa* in section 19 of *Being and Time*, and while he does examine Dasein's spatiality, he never goes into detail about how being an embodied entity is constitutive of Dasein itself.[2] I reply that this is not a mistake or a failing but rather a demonstration of how Heidegger's challenge of mind-body dualism operates. The characterization of Dasein is a challenge to traditional metaphysics that breaks down the "I" into various discrete parts (body, soul, and spirit) in order to get at the nature of human Being.[3] Contra the tradition, Heidegger asserts, "man's *'substance'* is not spirit as a synthesis of soul and body; it is rather *existence*."[4] It would be a mistake to think of Dasein as a compound or combination of body and mind/soul; Dasein is a whole unto itself, and its existence is what is relevant to Heidegger's fundamental ontology. The question "What is body?" would already presuppose dualism and the abstraction of the idea of body from the idea of self. But it is possible to think Dasein without having to abstract the idea of body from the idea of Dasein, and Heidegger does so throughout *Being and Time* when he describes Dasein as directional and oriented in-the-world, essentially embodied existence. The basic modes of Dasein's Being are being-in, being-alongside, being-in-space, being-with, being-toward, and being-there (*Da-sein*). It is not accidental that Heidegger uses so many terms that refer to spatial relationships when describing Dasein's Being. He presupposes and suggests physical relationships, even if metaphorically, precisely because Dasein understands its Being in terms of the physical. The body is Dasein's means of interaction with the world and the condition of its experiences. Meaningfulness is described in terms of distance and nearness: "When, for instance, a man wears a pair of spectacles which are so close to him distantially that they are 'sitting on his nose,' they are environmentally more remote from him than the picture on the opposite wall."[5] The picture is what matters; Dasein does not concern itself much with the glasses through which it observes the picture. Dasein, then, is fundamentally spatial, and its understanding of the world is neither a purely rational, disembodied kind of thinking nor mere sensory perception. Understanding is, rather, the way sensory perceptions matter to Dasein in-the-world.[6] The equipmental character of entities in the world is only possible because Dasein has a body with which to manipulate both equipment and the world. The characterization of Dasein, especially in section I.3 of *Being and Time*, is as a being fundamentally involved with the worldhood of the world. This is important, because Dasein is not merely a thinking thing; the world acts on Dasein in tangible ways, the physical world has the capacity to disclose or limit Dasein's ownmost potentiality for Being, and even Dasein's temporal Being is affected by its being physical. The past, which Dasein is at any given time projecting into the future, is experienced by means of the physical changes Dasein experiences. The world's operations on Dasein are possible precisely because Dasein's Being is embodied Being. So Heidegger actually gives an account of *embodied Dasein* while avoiding the reinscription of mind-body dualism that would be necessary if he were to give an account of *embodiment as such*.

Still, reading Heidegger in light of the history and context of phenomenology, incorporating Husserl, Merleau-Ponty, and Foucault, it becomes clear that a more robust account of Dasein's embodiment is possible. This is an admittedly idiosyncratic approach, but the focus of this inquiry is gender as a phenomenon and not any particular philosopher's body of work. For this reason, this chapter delves into (1) problems with Heidegger's account of Dasein as gender neutral, (2) Husserl's account of the body as the medium of perception and the function of norms in regard to intelligibility, (3) Merleau-Ponty's examination of sexual embodiment and freedom, and (4) Foucault's extensive analytics of discursive power. Once the contributions of these thinkers are incorporated into the considerations presented here, it is possible to (5) examine how gender is manifested in authentic and inauthentic Dasein.

At this point, it might be asked how the Dasein described in this book is even still Heidegger's Dasein.[7] In these pages, I trace Dasein from Heidegger's conception of how Being is experienced, through Husserl, Merleau-Ponty, Butler, and Foucault, focusing on gender and tinkering with technological orientations. So is this still Heidegger's Dasein and not, rather, something else? My reply is a stereotypical philosopher's "yes and no." This particular situation of Dasein is *one* Heideggerian model of human Being. We today do discuss and use Dasein differently than Heidegger did himself, because when he was alive and working, he did not have the benefit of the particular hindsight we now possess. His ideas had not yet accreted the past few decades of conceptual history. (And in another fifty years, there will be different Heideggerian readings still, because there will be another fifty years' worth of thought to read him through.) Heidegger did not read Aristotle as Aquinas did because he had the benefit of Aquinas's thought to influence his understanding. Heidegger was aware of this: "If Dasein's Being is in principle historical, then every factical science [*Wissenschaft*] is always manifestly in the grip of this historicizing."[8] Aside from carefully delineated thought experiments, ideas are never experienced as static or abstracted from the rest of the lived world. This includes, of course, Heidegger's own fundamental ontology. Nothing in experience is exempt from historicizing, including systems of thought that disclose historicity. Heidegger's work innovates on the history of Western thought, in particular the intractable knots of logic the Moderns tied themselves up with. His fundamental ontology is an innovation that is itself innovated on by others but is not obliterated or replaced in the process, any more than Aristotle's words are obliterated by the existence of Aquinas's.

Butler, Foucault, and Merleau-Ponty all make use of key features of Heidegger's Dasein and recast them in turn, whether they do so explicitly or implicitly. By the time these thinkers came on the scene, Heidegger's ideas were part of the Western philosophical zeitgeist. We can trace the heritage of the concept of gender as performative back to Heidegger's Dasein and his challenge of the subject-object distinction. Indeed, the conceptual history can be traced beyond that, through Husserl to the Modern search for the substantive self that Heidegger was responding to, but for the purposes of this particular inquiry, the conceptual link between Heidegger and Butler (and similar links between Heidegger and Merleau-Ponty, and Heidegger and Foucault) suffices. A history tracing the development of these concepts through various thinkers would be quite interesting, but that is a different project. The point of this book is to see how the *phenomenon* of gender can be examined, at center stage, and for that a collaborative approach is needed. The idea is not to read Heidegger through the lens of Merleau-Ponty through the lens of Foucault through the lens of Butler but to read these thinkers vertically (as one reads choral music), allowing points of harmony and dissonance to emerge and reveal insights about experience rather than textual analysis. This seems the most sensible approach for the phenomenologist interested in lived Being and intersections of meaningfulness precisely because it decenters text and theory and recenters experience. This Dasein is no strictly Heideggerian trope, pure and loyal to original text. The point of phenomenological inquiry is to delve into lived experience, which is always messy facticity. Phenomenology is no exception to the lived experience it examines. It too is subject to historical messiness, to development and innovation and thus to wide-reaching relevance as it is used to examine just about any topic of lived experience.

The Problem with Gendered Dasein

When it comes to gender, claims of Dasein's neutrality do not quite solve the problem of the role gender plays in Dasein's Being. Heidegger, in *The Metaphysical Foundations of Logic* and *Being and Time*, asserts the neutrality of Dasein with regard to gender. Is this position sustainable? What he seems to be trying to get at is what is fundamental to *all* cases of Dasein—not an entity that is neither male nor female but an entity that has the potentiality to be either. Gender difference does not appear to qualify, for Heidegger, as an ontological difference.[9] "The peculiar *neutrality* of the term 'Dasein' is essential, because the interpretation of this being must be carried out prior to every factual concretion."[10] This is problematic. Dasein is essentially an embodied entity; it is also an entity that is not taken as an isolated subject but as a being that is essentially *Mitsein*, and it is its facticity, never neutral or abstract.[11] And in *Being and Time*, Heidegger repeatedly asserts that Dasein is always already a particular Dasein.[12] Heidegger's insistence on Dasein's neutrality seems to mean that there must be something that preexists or is more primordial than Dasein's actual or factical Being-in-the-world, but this is a contradiction. Despite his assertion that neutral Dasein is not the "ontic, isolated individual"[13] of traditional metaphysics, he does not account for *what* this "proto-Dasein" is. He seems to be saying that Dasein is to be understood as an abstraction and, at the same time, that Dasein is *not* to be understood as an abstraction. There are a number of possible reconciliations to this contradiction: he could be adopting a Thomist model of matter—in this case, embodiment—as the individuating principle and speaking of Dasein as something akin to

Aristotelian-Thomistic form. He could be trying to express a conception of Dasein that is something other than factical Dasein, or he may be trying to discuss a characteristic that is common to all. None of these possibilities quite suffices, however, since they would require that Heidegger resort to a substantive self or a being that *becomes* Dasein, and this is contradictory to the description of Dasein as explicated in *Being and Time*.

The Thomist view on embodiment[14] is that the body, being material, is Dasein's individuating principle, and thus it is only on the physical level that Dasein is gendered. Although this would explain his insistence on discussing Dasein-as-such in *The Metaphysical Foundations of Logic*, it would seem not, since the Thomist model presupposes a division between body and soul that Heidegger rejects. And yet, in speaking of a neutral Dasein, the interpretation of which "must be carried out prior to every factual concretion,"[15] Heidegger would have to posit something akin to a preexisting soul or preexisting self that would have its Being prior to being individuated into a sexed body within a gender-conscious *Mitsein*, which he also rejects.[16]

Could it be that Heidegger is not talking about *factical* Dasein at all? This seems to me the most generous possible reading of the rare passages in which Heidegger discusses gender and sexuality. While such a reading is out of step with most of what Heidegger has to say about Dasein, it would account for his striking comments on the sexual and gender neutrality of Dasein. But then, what is there to say about nonfactical Dasein, given the following passage?

> In its neutrality Dasein is not the indifferent nobody and everybody, but the primordial positivity and potency of the essence. Neutrality is not the voidness of an abstraction, but precisely the potency of the *origin*, which bears in itself the intrinsic possibility of every concrete factual humanity.[17]

There is an outside possibility that in his characterization of Dasein as gender neutral, Heidegger is not talking about an abstract, and he is also not talking about a substantive self. There is perhaps something else at work here. Only a very naïve reading would take the word "origin," coming from Heidegger, to indicate a temporal origin. Instead, it can be taken more in the sense of the origin of a river, which feeds the river and which may branch off into one tributary or another. The foundational, primordial, and originary characteristic of Dasein, then, would be a type of Being that is differentiated into historical (or sexed and gendered) Dasein. So Heidegger's point might be that just as there is a commonality to all cases of Dasein, regardless of their specific historicality, there is also a similar commonality to all instances of Dasein, regardless of their specific sex and gender.[18]

Even this is not a successful claim, however. In his characterization of Dasein, Heidegger makes claim to a universality that he may not be able to support. As Derrida points out in his essay "Geschlecht: Sexual Difference, Ontological Difference," once sexuality is neutralized, there is a risk of repeating the error of traditional philosophy, which denies sexual difference and in so doing reinforces the established tradition of regarding the male as the only "true" sex, defining the female only in terms of the male or as a flawed version of the male.[19] As Tina Chanter has noted, Heidegger's descriptions of Dasein are very specific to a kind of human being:

> Heidegger's Dasein is one who is largely untroubled by its bodily existence (except insofar as bodily needs are subordinated to goal-oriented ends, as in the for-the-sake-of-which), one who assumes the priority of self over other, and one for whom spatiality is subordinated to temporal ordering. Is it accidental that all these facets of Dasein's existence articulate traditionally masculine characteristics?[20]

In other words, in the very assumptions he makes about the character of Dasein, it can be seen that Heidegger does indeed take a stance on Dasein's gender, whether he intends to or not, simply by not examining the privileging of the masculine that underlies most Western assumptions. (It is no accident that the word for "man" in almost every European language is also the word for "human being.") By positing Dasein as a being whose existence is fundamentally masculine, without taking a reflective stance on this positing, Heidegger perpetuates the traditional conception of human being as male. He falls prey to the obscuring insensitivity toward difference that *das Man* routinely exercises, and this is precisely why he never gets to the "heart of the matter"[21] regarding gender. This omission renders Dasein anything but universal. Heidegger's fundamental ontology simply fails to address significant phenomenal aspects of one half of all cases of Dasein. Furthermore, it leaves little room for addressing social and political injustice. If Dasein is understood from the outset as neutral, there is no way of addressing the very real differences between individuals that Dasein does encounter in the lived world, whether they be sexual, gender-related, racial, economic, or classist.[22]

The description of Dasein's stance with regard to gender as "neutral" is a dead end; it just does not cohere. Dasein is assuredly *factical*, however, and this term does a much better job of describing how gender operates. "Neutrality" suggests detachment and impartiality. Dasein is anything but detached and impartial. Dasein is *Mitsein*, always particular, always partial, always perspectival, always engaged with the world and with others. It would seem that, to one degree or another, gender is a function of *Mitsein*. After all, one cannot speak of gender or sexual difference without presupposing an Other. Types do not exist unless there are at least two exemplars: one that fits the type and one that does not. Gender expression and identity are culturally determined, and Dasein's Being is ordinarily immersed in *das Man*, the culturally determining, public, inauthentic mode of Dasein's *Mitsein*. Dasein has the tendency to interpret its own experiences in terms of the context and perspective that it absorbs from *das Man*, according to its relation to others, at least as long as it remains in the everyday fallen mode. It makes sense that gender, which amounts to cultural classification of Dasein into types and the understanding of how these types relate to one another, would be a function of *das Man* and thus of *Mitsein*. For instance, I am a man because I am not a woman, and the expectation (predicated on the body with which I was born) that I be a woman was problematic, provoking the transition from one gender role to another. My fulfillment of the role of "man" in my culture is thus dependent on my assumption of this culture's particular, historical conception of "masculinity" at this time. And what of biological sex? In this regard, biology is to a great extent a function of *Mitsein* as well, since scientific endeavors are shaped by cultural needs and presuppositions. It could be that the difference between sex and gender is loosely analogous to the distinction Heidegger makes in *Origin of the Work of Art* between earth and world. Earth is the material existence of entities, whereas world is the context of their meaningfulness to Dasein.[23] Sex (or at any rate, the sexual properties of bodies) is more or less biological fact, but what this biological fact means is often translated into gender, which, in return, renders biological fact intelligible. Furthermore, gender, as *Geschlecht*, can mean much more than mere sexual difference. Since it applies to types of Dasein, *Geschlecht* could easily be translated in social discourse to differences such as class, socioeconomic position, skin color, or even body size and attractiveness. Any aspect of Dasein's facticity that is drawn from *Mitsein* and has to do with the way Dasein's Being is played out in the social sphere might be seen as having to do with *Geschlecht*. For this reason, the question of gender in terms of social expectations that attach more or less strictly to biological sex is every bit as urgent to Dasein's Being as questions of class struggle, race, or social justice. Indeed, gender can be understood only in terms of how it intersects with various other *Geschlechter*, including age, race, and class.

Heidegger, as the philosopher interested in the everyday, has left quite a puzzle to work out regarding Dasein and gender. There are contradictions in his work that raise questions, but there also is in Dasein a very useful model for exploring the question of gender in more depth, one that allows the phenomenologist to bypass many of the contradictions and logical snarls encountered by the Western philosophical tradition. It provides a minimalist model of experience and a phenomenological method that acknowledges and addresses the difficulties of a perspectival approach to this issue. The model of Dasein allows for claims about gender with as few metaphysical presuppositions as possible and forces acknowledgement of the role these presuppositions play in the way gender has arisen as a problem to be addressed. The aim is not to gain a God's-eye perspective on some universal facet of human nature but rather to gain *a* perspective, while retaining intellectual integrity by acknowledging that this perspective is one of many possible perspectives. There is a great deal that is unknown about human experience. This much is known: people are here, are embodied beings, are involved in a social and historical context, are individuals, and are the beings to whom their own Being matters. Using Dasein as a starting point for an exploration of gender provides the advantage of avoiding the pitfalls presented by systems that take more than Being-there-with-others for granted. If this is to be effective, Dasein's experience of the body must be investigated in greater depth.

Husserl

Husserl, Heidegger's mentor, provides a significant account of the phenomenon of embodiment, identifying the body as "*the medium of all perception*; it is the *organ of perception* and is *necessarily* involved in all perception. . . . [T]here is also given the fact that, on this original foundation, all that is thingly-real in the surrounding world of the Ego has its relation to the Body."[24] The body is how objects are encountered; the world is oriented in relation to the body. The book is *before* me, while the window is *to my right*. And since the body is deployed in the world, the manner of that deployment will determine the manner of the individual's being. Without a body, there could be no consciousness of objects, which constitute the meaningful world. Perception, then, is reliant on embodiment. But the world is made up of much more than mere raw perception. Perceptions are more or less intelligible as they are recognized as occurring within (or contradicting) a context of meaningfulness, as part of a lived world. Things are given in perception and become intelligible as a kind of abstraction from perception. The normal, or what tends to be expected, is used as a reference by which the perception is measured. The silver-and-white object over which my fingers are moving, causing electrical impulses to communicate ones and zeroes to a machine, is only understandable in a world in which keyboards and computers exist, are known, and matter. When something unknown is encountered, there is a tendency to seek familiar, "normal" aspects of it to make sense of what it is, how it works, and why it matters.

The normal is neither a universal nor a particular. It acts as a touchstone or standard against which particular perceptions are measured and understood. The normal can change as the particular situation in which it functions may vary. The normal is

> in the series of possible appearances a certain givenness of the thing [that is] privileged in that with it is given, *of the thing as a whole, what is relatively the best*, and this acquires the character of what is *especially intended*: it is the predominating focus of the "interest," what the *experience is tending toward, terminates in,* is fulfilled in; and the other modes of givenness become intentionally related to this "optimal" one.[25]

This is to say that the normal is the form of any thing that allows it to be identifiable, the perception of which changes as the body's relation to it changes. This is not an ethical claim, although the language Husserl uses here can easily be conflated with the language of normative ethics.[26] Basically, the "normal" is what remains the same, the most objective, throughout the various changes in various perceptions of some thing. It is optimal because it is the most reliably "there"; it is what remains behind the obstructed or alterable view of a thing. It is the "real" color of the writing table I want to buy, when it is not viewed under the fluorescent light of the store, for instance.

The normal functions as a means of creating common intelligibility among individuals, who all have distinct perceptions of any given object. If there are ten people in a room, and all ten people have a different perspective of an object in the room—say, a writing table—then how is it that all ten people can be said to see the "same" table? Because one "can furthermore assume that all the persons who have commerce with one another apprehend the world completely alike (abstraction made from the always necessary differences in orientation)."[27] That is, all ten see the same writing table because all ten have an abstracted, normalized idea of what a writing table is. So perceptions are private, but abstractions based on perceptions are very much a public phenomenon and one by which all ten may make their perceptions intelligible to one another. The discussion of a particular writing table makes use of several abstractions and the table's greater or lesser conformity to the norms expressed by the abstractions. The table's haecceity (its "this-ness," or distinction as an individual from the type) is perceived as its relation to the norm, to what is expected of such a table in this particular context. If it is I who purchased the table, it will have been clawed by a cat within an hour of having been brought into my home. Thus, *this* table (type) will be *cat-clawed* (individuating feature) and *in my home* (individuating feature).

This is a contingent state of affairs because it is only as long as a norm functions in this way that it can be made use of as a norm, and a norm is only itself intelligible in contrast to abnormalities.[28] This is crucial: an abnormality or anomaly is that which stands out as contradictory to what is expected or understood as a norm. Of course, the phenomenal world is not an ideal world of abstractions but, rather, a lived world of encounters with particulars. And particulars are always anomalies; they are always understood in terms of a particular orientation to them. Even if two objects with no perceptible differences are presented to a person, it will always be the case that they will have different relations to that person's body in space. Two writing tables may appear almost exactly alike, but one will have a different orientation to the body than the other will, standing to the left of the other, perhaps. Abstraction and norms are insufficient to account for lived experience. "Anomalies" will always appear as a result of interaction with a physical world.[29] Embodied orientation in relation to objects described and understood in abstract terms is precisely what makes the world and the objects in it intelligible, even when objects are otherwise indistinguishable from one another.

How can Husserl's analysis apply to the question of gender? If abnormality is a contradiction of the normal, which itself functions as a nexus of intelligibility, what is to be made of atypical bodies? Of atypically sexed bodies? Of atypical genders? Is there some model of the human body that can be understood as being "normal" or "objectively the best?" If so, what version is it, and how is such a body gendered? And if, as Husserl says, the abnormal always reverts back to the normal when the impediments preventing normal perception are removed,[30] why is it that norms change? This question is important; just by being asked, it reveals that norms are perceptual, not universal. It is obvious that what is considered normal in one place or historical period may well be regarded as anomalous in another. Since it seems that Husserl is referring to the norm as the essential characteristics of any given thing, would it be correct to say that a body that is statistically anomalous is, in fact, in a state that could be called, for *this* body, "normal"? Would a transgender individual, statistically anomalous, be "normal" when engaged in what are, for her, ordinary activities, and anomalous only when she does something unusual? Husserl does not answer anything like this question, of course, but the question is one that raises the issue of whether gender is an essential characteristic capable of being thought of as a phenomenal norm and, if so, whether it is an essential characteristic of *individuals* or of *cultures*. Husserl simply does not address this question, so Merleau-Ponty's and Foucault's theories regarding sexual difference and how such differences are articulated in discourse come in very handy.

Merleau-Ponty

Maurice Merleau-Ponty gives an account of embodiment that turns the traditional conception of soul as residing in the body around and claims instead that the body is found within the self. As he says, to "look at the object is to plunge oneself into it."[31] To be sure, the way the self experiences the world is by means of the body, but the self extends, through perception, beyond the confines of the body itself to the world. What Merleau-Ponty offers to this project is an examination of sexual embodiment. Human being is sexual. Where Freud both noticed the importance of sexuality in human life and attributed a significant amount of actions to sexual motivations, Merleau-Ponty agrees that sexuality is a special and very significant aspect of human being but also asks which is the primary, more primordial motivation and signifier of meaningfulness for human being: sexuality or existentiality?[32] His answer is neither but rather that sexuality is so important and meaningful to the human condition that

> there is an interfusion between sexuality and existence, which means that existence permeates sexuality and *vice versa*, so that it is impossible to determine, in a given decision or action, the proportion of sexual to other motivations, impossible to label a decision or act "sexual" or "non-sexual."[33]

In other words, there is so much sexual content to nonsexual actions and so much nonsexual content to sexual actions that it is impossible to separate the two aspects of life into tidy compartments. There is, rather, an overall omnipresence of sexuality that is inspired by its own meaningfulness in the phenomenal world and also constitutive of that meaningfulness in that it directs human activity.[34] The sexual aspects of an individual act as both cause and effect; sexuality can cause a certain deportment in the world, and having a certain deportment in the world can affect one's sexuality.[35]

Now, since Merleau-Ponty holds that the body is not separate from the self, or something the self has, but rather that "I am my body,"[36] embodiment itself must be sexual and not only sexual but also *sexed* and gendered. Whereas the Western tradition, including Freud, regards biological sex as stable and indicative of gender, Merleau-Ponty takes a very interesting approach to this issue. He regards being a man or a woman as a kind of *style* of embodied being: "Thus sexuality and, more generally, corporeality . . . is a power of investment which is absolute and universal to begin with. This power is *sexual* only in the sense that it reacts immediately to the visible differences of the body and the maternal and paternal roles."[37] The sex of the body of another is, then, part of immediate and unmediated perception, "a certain manner of being flesh that is given entirely."[38] Such immediate correspondence to others is available because the boundaries of the self are, in fact, permeable by the boundaries of other selves.[39] (People use our bodies to perceive other people's bodies.) In practice, access to another person's biological sex is nearly always gendered access—other people's primary sex characteristics are rarely directly visible. Gender performance creates expectations regarding biological sex and personal history, and it is freely accessed in everyday interactions. Gendered expectations may or may not be borne out by fact, but the only way that the styles of being identified as male and female (or masculine and feminine) can be intelligible is within a world that already provides the means of understanding given styles *as already being* masculine and feminine. Sexual identity, then, is not accounted for merely by biology. Essential properties of bodies, which are rarely visible, also do not account for it. What does account for identity is the social context in which individuals find themselves situated at any given time and the meaningfulness that particular forms of embodiment have. A woman is identifiable as a woman because she performs femininity in various ways, which allows her to occupy the social role of woman. Sexuality, the body's sex, and gender are all conditions that constitute the possibility of the operation of freedom.[40]

Merleau-Ponty's exegesis on freedom is a departure from the classical questions regarding freedom and determinism and takes a broader approach to the issue, conceiving of freedom as a kind of exchange between the self and the field of possibilities that are afforded by the lived world. Freedom is not, at its foundation, the mere choice between P and Q but the very conditions that allow for the possibility to make such a choice, the structures that enable the possibility of choice to exist at all.[41] Embodied selves are the seat of the world's appearance and meaningfulness. It is bodies' particular orientation in the world that creates individual possibilities in the way bodies interrelate with objects and both find and establish meaningfulness. Objects act on people, to be sure, but people also act on objects. So freedom occurs only within a given situation but is also self-directed. Living humans never do just nothing, so freedom is the freedom to choose one project, one theme, one style, one life, or another in the world. And the natural world is nothing other than the field of possibility for "all possible themes and styles."[42] Themes and styles, including biological sex, gender, and sexuality, are enacted, embodied, and lived within a world in which they are intelligible and meaningful. All the world's a stage for living themes and styles in particular ways; there is no "backstage" in which styles are first set and then performed—the public stage is the workshop of style. This, then, is the activity of freedom: people always already find themselves situated in a meaningful world, shaped by history and their own past, in which particular choices are presented (and these are not always the choices people would prefer!). At the same time, choices themselves constitute the world in the present and with an eye toward the future.

Foucault

To begin, a simple fact: a discourse becomes dominant because it succeeds. By "succeeds," I do not mean "is good" or "is to be desired by an ethical agent." Many discourses that succeed are ones I would very much like to see replaced. I mean much the same thing that a biologist might describe as a species' thriving: when a discourse "succeeds," it manages to perpetuate itself and continue to shape the world, even as it alters in response to pressures placed on it by other phenomena in its environment. Economic systems, languages, and religious iconographies are examples of discourses that thrive. To be sure, a great many discourses thrive at the expense of some members of the culture they shape. Racism, sexism, economic inequality all "succeed" in the sense that they perpetuate themselves throughout historical vicissitudes, altering as the climate requires, but this does not mean that they *ought* to be perpetuated. What is operative in the rise of a particular discourse is not primarily logical necessity, or even correspondence of statements to actual fact, but the way a discourse is shaped by its presuppositions and expectations. If the very constitutions of fact and truth are a result of discourse, as Foucault has it (and I agree), then all truth comes down to cohesion with the discourses available to be utilized in experiencing and understanding phenomena that are experienced. If a particular discourse does not succeed, if it does not provide an intelligible context according to which experience can be understood, it does not thrive. So those discourses that Foucault describes as being successful ones, such as religion, medicine, and law, perform some kind of function that not only guarantees their own self-perpetuation but also says something meaningful about human experience.[43] To contrast, phrenology is an example of a discourse that failed to sustain its meaningfulness. Once it was established that the bumps found on the skull lack correlation with criminal tendencies, people stopped taking phrenology seriously; there simply was not enough cultural commitment to the practice to guarantee its evolving into a more useful sort of discourse. The real power of the discourses Foucault describes as being successful is that they set the standards of proof and identify for the relevant aspects of phenomena that individuals undertake to examine. They are like the rules of perspective, which may differ from one culture to another but set up the possibility of creating paintings that more or less truthfully represent the world. Dominant discourses do not tell people what to think, but they tell people what to think about, and how to think about it. In this sense, discourses of knowledge and power shape the world itself; they are precisely the field in which Merleau-Ponty's conception of freedom is played out. Furthermore, discourses of power "work" when they are, to one degree or another, coherent with the possibilities and limitations presented by the physical world and the body, however these are constructed and understood. How phenomena can be talked about amounts to the establishment of what is possible within a field of discourse.

Discourses do change, as history demonstrates. This is important: discourses are not immutable Truths that can never be contravened. While discourses of power are operating on human beings, indeed *disciplining* human beings into a shape that makes sense, at the same time, human beings are operating on and disciplining those very institutions of power. In Foucault's archaeology, members of a society perpetuate normative discourses and disciplines on bodies and on members of the society. This includes themselves. In their operations of power, institutions create systems in which citizens employ self-discipline to perpetuate the truths generated by the discourses of power. But then, if this is happening, it must be the case that individuals are affecting these institutions in return, presenting them with needs to be met and difficulties to be overcome. This means that individuals find themselves already constituted in and by a matrix of power discourses and also that the individual is a component of the constitution of those power discourses and has the power to initiate changes in them.[44] This is where the phenomenon of transgender experience both challenges and reinscribes gender norms. As a transsexual man, I find myself living within a culture that is strongly invested in the maintenance of gender norms. My very existence and visibility operate as a challenge to these norms. I am simultaneously engaged in perpetuating gender norms, in that I have taken the identity and social role understood as "man," and challenging them by having switched from my former (failed) attempts to identify as a "woman." In choosing to live out of the closet, I make people think about what it is they expect of me with regard to gender. In doing so, I engage in a kind of simultaneous perpetuation of and challenge to the discourse that governs who is to be regarded as a man and who is to be regarded as a woman.[45]

One way in which the discourse of power has undergone changes is the way valuing happens. In one of his early works, "A Preface to Transgression," Foucault examines how the dominant discourse regarding sexuality arose in light of Nietzsche's declaration of the death of God. Nietzsche's God is the Western world's notion of an all-powerful, all-knowing, perfect being. Such a being is, according to the Western tradition, inconceivable by the imperfect human mind. Yet it is an imperfect understanding of this being's will and qualities, an imagining of his perfection, that has for millennia been the rule by which all that is knowable is measured. The truth-value of any matter has been compared to the imagined perfection of God and judged accordingly. Historically, this conception of God has operated as the discourse that provides a goal for mankind's enterprises. Every human endeavor has been an attempt to draw nearer to God's perfection. Thus, it can be argued that mankind has pushed its ability further and in a more focused manner than it would have had it lacked such a goal. Scientific and technological advancements, in seeking a single, unified truth, have vastly increased the quality of human life. The more closely any matter has conformed to the imagined perfection of God, the more truthful it has been thought to be. However, every human experience, under this system, falls short of the very type of truth sought. Since truth has been associated with perfection, goodness has been determined by the degree to which a matter in question can be said to be true. That is, goodness is determined by conformity to God. Furthermore, it has been assumed that God is a rational entity and that there must therefore be some rhyme and reason to all that exists, that Being must certainly follow some divine plan, and that any apparently random or chaotic event only seems so, because of mankind's imperfect understanding of divine nature.

In saying that God is dead, then, Nietzsche claims far more than that the life has gone out of a previously vital entity. His point is that human beings are no longer willing to accept such chimerical notions as the standard by which the tangible experiences of their lives are to be judged, and this inability to achieve the perfection of God no longer operates as a limit on human being. Instead, humankind is ready to acknowledge that there is no absolutely perfect measure by which goodness and truth can be gauged. This is a frightening concept. Human beings' chief tool and weapon in the world is reason. The death of God amounts to the admission that there is no single reasonable explanation for the world or any event that takes place in it. This is not to say that there are no standards at all, only that none of them is absolute. What is known as a gallon today may not equal an ounce tomorrow and a pint next Tuesday, but what measures as a gallon in the United States does not equal a gallon in United Kingdom. Standards do exist, but they change as their contexts change. When circumstances change in a way that causes standards to hinder rather than benefit human thriving, they must be modified to suit these new circumstances or be abandoned. In announcing the death of God, Nietzsche claims that a standard of imagined perfection, of which all human experience must necessarily fall short and be defined by its limit *as* a falling-short, has outlasted its value to humanity and must be abandoned.

In light of the death of God, which is the denial of "the limit of the Limit-less,"[46] a challenge arises to rethink how valuing occurs. As Foucault's later studies show, one of the conditions of valuing today is in terms of sexuality, a phenomenon that has emerged over the past few centuries, proliferating a vocabulary and grammar and becoming part of the language used to express the experience of being human. "Sexuality is only decisive for our culture as it is spoken, and to the degree it is spoken."[47] Religion and sexuality share the common element of excess;[48] religious fervor and sexual rapture share an ecstatic quality. In the wake of God's death, phenomenologists have turned inward to explore the limits placed on Being, limits that are, quite literally, the limits by which experience is defined, or rendered finite and thus intelligible. Foucault argues that these limits are made known by means of transgression. Transgression is disclosive; it shows the limits, and the limits delineate the transgression. Thus, not only does transgression do violence to the established order, but it also illuminates the structure of the order itself.

> The limit and transgression depend on each other for whatever density of be-ing they possess: a limit could not exist if it were absolutely uncrossable and, reciprocally, transgression would be pointless if it merely crossed a limit composed of illusions and shadows.[49]

The established order could not be appreciated *as* order unless there were transgressions to disclose it. And, of course, without such an order, transgression would not be possible; there would be nothing to transgress. In fact, in the case of transgressive sexuality, homosexuality historically came to be understood prior to heterosexuality; as a pathology, a perceived transgression of the established order, homosexuality cast the heterosexual into sharp focus and made it articulable, whereas before it had simply been assumed.[50]

In short, Foucault's account of body has little to do with material substance and everything to do with its being a pole around which power is deployed. The body itself is constituted by the discourses that take place about it. Any understanding of the body is shaped by how the body is talked about, and these discourses are historical processes that are contingent and cumulative of the historical presuppositions they propagate or challenge. And such challenges do take place: transgressions of the normal order, which is consonant with the dominant discourse, do occur. This happens quite often, as medical discoveries are made and as new forms of transgression emerge that illuminate the limits established by the dominant discourse.

There are individuals who find their own embodied experience at odds with the dominant discourses' declarations of what is true. This raises the question: What is going on in the operations of power where such individuals are concerned, if not the generation of discourse by means of transgression? The more unexpected variations humans produce, the more discourses are generated. It is not only that power is produced and reinforced by discourse but that discourse "also undermines and exposes [power], renders it fragile and makes it possible to thwart it."[51] To be sure, the transgressive individual is always already within the power operations of discourse and thus utilizes the language of discourse itself. But this is nothing new; this is how discourses of power operate. The transgressive power of discourse is also always already available to the individual. This happens within the language of intelligibility, but it does indeed happen. As Foucault points out, "Homosexuality began to speak in its own behalf . . . using the same categories by which it was medically disqualified."[52] Later, homosexual activists put an end to that medical disqualification and turned toward speaking out against legal and social disqualification, with remarkably swift success in some areas, at least as compared to other civil rights movements. Other types of transgression operate in a similar manner, building on the foundation of earlier transgressions that have been rendered intelligible. Now that homosexuality is no longer "unspeakable," trans issues are coming to the fore of public discourse; more and more of various types of transgression are showing up on the scene, sometimes much to the dismay of gays and lesbians.[53]

Discourse has the power to express truths or norms only in the presence of contradictions to the rule. Normality is defined by the medical community as that which is opposite of pathology. As the medical discourses of the eighteenth and nineteenth centuries produced more and more varieties of sexual pathology, they also gave birth to the sexual norm.[54] The idea of the norm is intelligible only when contrasted to what transgresses the norm, so transgressors of the norm have always been part of the operation of power through discourse. If there is no challenge to a state of affairs, there is no discourse about it, and if there is no discourse, norms cannot be articulated and established. Laws and taboos are enacted not against things that have not created a problem for the norm sometime in history but rather in response to those that present a problem for the operations of power. Indeed, this is the only way the operation of power can itself be intelligible: heteronormativity, like all normativities, thrives on the actual existence of those who transgress its dictates and peskily assert its contingency.

The potential for those individuals who transgress the norm to alter the face of the dominant discourses of power is built into the power dynamic itself. Multiple discourses are in operation at any given time.[55] It follows from this that all bodies, not only those that do not fit the norm, are engaged in this dynamic. This means that individuals, who are constituted by discourses of power, have the capacity to affect the deployment of power on themselves and in the discursive field at large. Since the Stonewall riots, the discourse that makes sense of individual rights has been taking over from those discourses that used to allow the exclusion of homosexuals to make sense.

This is significant because Foucault's exegesis of the development of sexuality as a historical construct describes how power is deployed to create social norms and cultural contexts. He describes the nuts and bolts of the operations of *das Man* and its relation to Dasein, although he does not explicitly use Heidegger's model or language. Where Heidegger describes the effect *das Man* has on Dasein and fallenness, Foucault describes how *das Man* undergoes the operations that have this effect. Gender is one such construct of *das Man* and is very closely related to sex and sexuality precisely because this is how the dominant discourse has defined all three. It is this discourse that lends intelligibility to Beauvoir's famous dictum, "One is not born, but rather becomes, a woman."[56] Gender is assigned on the basis of biological (and usually merely genital) classifications of sex but also carries with it a great deal more baggage than mere biology. If sexuality as an aspect of human identity is constructed by institutional discourse and deployments of power, then the deployment of genders, as classifications of persons in terms of biology, social expectations, and personal understanding of self, is an even more complex but no less *cohesive* construction. This means that gender is every bit as prone to reify perceptual and cultural norms that are established by transgression as sexuality is.

So, whereas Heidegger only vaguely sketches out the broad strokes of Dasein's embodiment, Husserl, Merleau-Ponty, and Foucault fill in many of the details Heidegger left out of his picture. It may be helpful to restate these theories in terms of Heidegger's theory of Dasein and *Mitsein* in order to more efficiently seat them within the discussion at hand. For Husserl, the body is the condition of perception; objects and the world are encountered by means of the body and in relation to the body. The body itself, then, will determine the kind of being a given Dasein has, by determining its very possibility of comportment and orientation in regard to the world. Perceptions constitute the basis of what is understood by consciousness; they both shape and respond to the context of meaningfulness that is the lived world. For the world to be intelligible, there must be some kind of common intelligibility, and norms function as the means of establishing this common intelligibility among individuals' private perceptions. Since each Dasein has a distinct set of perceptions of any given object, consciousness perceives not only its own private sense data of any given object in the world but also the norm of the thing, what seems to remain the same or the most easily shared, throughout the various differences in the perceptions of any thing experienced by various cases of Dasein. Norms are not necessarily normative, although they can be. What is interesting about norms is that they function as the point of reference by which any particular Dasein's private perceptions can be measured and evaluated. The "real Being" of the world, then, is not posited as a transcendent *Ding an sich* or as a Cartesian substance but rather as immediate perception by means of the body that is always oriented toward meaningful intersubjectivity. Dasein's particular embodiment, then, is the means of its being always already situated *in* a world and of its constitution *of* the world.

Merleau-Ponty expands on Husserl's work regarding embodiment with his accounts of sexual embodiment and freedom. Sexuality is a special form of Dasein's Being in the Western culture of the twenty-first century because it interfuses with existence in such a way that it is impossible to meaningfully separate Dasein's Being from its sexuality; sexuality is always already present, as both the source of meaningfulness Dasein finds in the world and as the motivation for Dasein's constitution of the world. Biological sex and sexuality are styles of Being for Merleau-Ponty, and they are constituted not only by biology but also by *Mitsein*. Dasein's sexuality is important because it is important to *das Man*. People really do want to know who is gay and who is not, who is a man and who is a woman. This phenomenon is a function of how social constructions of gender and sexuality have come to be understood as foundational to Dasein's Being. (It is in the relationships Dasein finds itself situated in at any given time that sexual identity is situated, because both biological sex and sexuality are intelligible in terms of social constructs.) The field of possibility for Dasein's Being to be of a particular style, such as male or female, masculine or feminine, is what Merleau-Ponty characterizes as freedom, which is acting or living the choices presented within a particular factical situation in-the-world, within a particular body, and within a particular history.

Where both Husserl and Merleau-Ponty flesh out Heidegger's account of embodiment, Foucault's account of the body as intelligible only through discourse provides the means of examining how *das Man* operates on Dasein's embodied Being. Discourses of power orient Dasein's Being-in-the-world and Being-with-others in an intelligible way by providing the common ground of intelligibility within which Dasein operates. Most of the time, institutions of power operate *on* Dasein, and particularly on Dasein's body. This is, of course, what is happening when Dasein is in the mode of fallenness. Fallen Dasein submits to the disciplines enjoined by *das Man*, and it is this submission that makes the ordinary, everyday world intelligible to Dasein. Fallen Dasein understands the world in terms of dominant institutional discourses of law, of custom, of the church, and so on, which exercise their power over it, and orients itself bodily to conform to the norms espoused by the discourses. *Das Man* is nothing if not a disciplining power over Dasein and, in fact, one that causes Dasein to engage in self-discipline. One of the final straws in my own coming-out process was when I realized I had changed position to sit in a more "ladylike" manner, sacrificing comfort to do so, while alone in my own home. The power of discourse to shame Dasein into self-policing behavior can be surprisingly compelling. But the power of discourse is not limited to fallen Dasein. Dominant discourses of power provide the context and the vocabulary for Dasein's occasional authenticity. When a dominant discourse ceases for whatever reason to be *zuhanden* and instead becomes *vorhanden*[57] to Dasein, it becomes conspicuous, and Dasein engages with it in an authentic manner. When this happens, Dasein is no longer only operated on by institutions of discourse but rather becomes the agent operating on the discourse itself, by questioning and at times transgressing the norms that establish intelligibility in the world. A switch in the power dynamic occurs, and Dasein becomes an active participant in the constitution of its world. In the case of sitting in the "right way," I began to examine the compulsion to ladylike behavior but also my own identification and what it was costing me to try to conform to a style for which I was simply not equipped. The cost was enormous; the energy expended in enduring perpetual discomfort is difficult for those who have never experienced it to fathom. The price of constant blows to self-confidence, self-policing, and second-guessing turned out to be much higher than the efforts required for transitioning. (This applies to my relatively privileged case. I should be clear, however, that this reckoning includes the dangers posed by violent and nonviolent opposition to my existence.) I began shortly thereafter to live as a man and thus began to actively challenge the Western understanding of gender simply by thriving.

The divorce of gender from biological sex is an example of a Foucauldian switch: the visibility of gender transgressive cases of Dasein has the potential to cause a "breakdown" of the discourse that creates an expectation that bio-logical sex and gender will "match up" in certain ways. What the increasing visibility of gender transgressors shows is that the expectation that all mem-bers of a given biological sex will always behave in a certain gendered manner and will be of a particular sexual orientation is unreasonable. The expectation, demonstrated unreasonable, thus comes under scrutiny. Norms and intelligi-bility of factical life are reliant on contexts of meaningfulness in which gender plays an enormous role. Dasein literally orients its body—its medium of per-ception—in different ways when interacting with those of different genders. The norms by which Dasein measures its perceptions of others are almost al-ways involved with gender, insofar as certain types of bodies engender certain expectations of behavior and a sense of uncanniness when these expectations are not met. Sometimes this failure to meet expectations results in violent op-position, the destruction of gender transgressive individuals. But in aggregate, like erosion, it results in adjustment of society's expectations.

Authentic Dasein, Transgressive Dasein

Speaking of society's expectations, Dasein is characterized in *Being and Time* as having two primary modes of Being, authenticity and fallenness. For the most part, Dasein is fallen in-the-world-with-others, concerned with the un-reflective tasks of its everyday life. At times, however, Dasein is faced with its ownmost potentiality for authenticity and is called to take a different ap-proach to its own Being—that is, to take responsibility for understanding its life as a coherent whole. Sometimes the cause of this call to authenticity is the fact that unequal social conditions can force an intolerable "uncanniness" on Dasein, which makes it impossible to remain comfortably and unreflectingly within the familiar, everyday world.

Heidegger's description of fallen Dasein as everyday, unreflective Dasein absorbed in concern for the world, immersed in *das Man* and ways of thinking that are culturally determined and public, is seminal. These ways of thinking are what Foucault calls "discourses of power," paradigms for how people think of the world and relationships with others. On the negative side, discourses of power may be banal mental habits that enable Dasein to be lazy in its think-ing, perpetrating stereotypes and ignoring oppressions. On the positive side, they can provide terms and contexts for new ways of thinking out the concrete situations in which Dasein finds itself. In both cases, what is at issue is that the ways of thinking and speaking of phenomena are produced not by individuals but by social institutions and *das Man*. Such scripts and discourses of power are essential to Dasein because they provide the very language with which meaningful encounters between individuals can be performed and described; they are foundational to the ways Dasein's Being-with is constituted, by serving as the field in which common intelligibility is made possible. However, there are always already multiple scripts or discourses of power operating in any given culture. Even if Dasein always already understands itself as being part of *das Man*, particular conceptions are not fixed or universal. There are many choices available for any fallen Dasein to live its life, so even in its fallen state, Dasein is not strictly identical to *das Man* or to fallen others. It is simply the case that fallen Dasein is in its default state of Being, and its choices are made within the scope of those possibilities provided by *das Man*.

The only thing some may find "wrong" with fallenness is that in its fallen state Dasein does not seek to actualize its potential in its ownmost Being-in-the-world. Fallen Dasein is everyday Dasein, who dresses, speaks, and behaves as it is expected to do, without thought or question, since it is caught up in everyday concern with tasks and relatively short-term projects. Authentic Dasein, on the other hand, is concerned with achieving "coherence, cohesiveness, and integrity [in] a life course."[58] To achieve authenticity, Dasein has to "own" its own life. To take charge of its own life, Dasein must, at least temporarily, leave the comfortable position it holds in *das Man* and strike out on its own into the very uncomfortable uncanniness of individuation. This is a daunting proposition, for while *das Man* necessarily limits the scope of Dasein's possibility, it also is precisely what constitutes the intelligibility of that very same possibility. To achieve authenticity is to risk comfort and a given understanding of Dasein's position in-the-world-with-others. Indeed, it is to risk its own understanding of the world itself and to thrust itself into new territory, into its own potentiality for being a "whole person." When Dasein experiences authentically, new modes of meaningfulness are established, and Dasein is able to view its life as a coherent whole, instead of merely as a string of tasks to be completed and obstacles to be overcome in day-to-day life. This is not to say that Dasein must be a coherent *subject*, in the tradition of Western philosophy—Dasein is not a thing and need not itself be coherent—but only that *this* life course makes sense as distinct from others, with causal relationships based in experience. Of course, all this happens in response to discourses that are still, after a fashion, dominant, and it is such discourses that the current project aims to elucidate. In the sense that they are reacting to the dominant perspective, even the most revolutionary authentic perspectives are part and parcel of the dominant perspective. Authenticity is conscious variation on the themes that are taken for granted by fallen Dasein, themes that open up the possibility that Dasein may create new perspectives in order to take responsibility for its own Being and live its life in a way that more fully realizes its ownmost potential for self-actualization.

Just how *does* Dasein manage to take an authentic stance? There really is not a how-to manual for this. (Any manual would quickly become the very type of social convention that fosters fallenness.) Dasein, in addition to being-with-others, is historical, and is thus bound by a past that determines its destiny, a destiny that is "co-historizing and is determinative for"[59] Dasein's Being. However, Dasein is no mere automaton at the mercy of its historical situation; rather, it is an active participant in its own history and *Mitsein*, insofar as it exercises choice over those aspects of its culture in which it may choose to ground its resoluteness. One way this happens is seizing on the possibility that Dasein can choose a hero, which is to say, Dasein can focus on another, using that other as a model on which to structure its own life.[60] In doing so, Dasein does not become the hero but rather shapes its own life according to what it believes the other might be or might have been. When Dasein chooses to repeat the possibility for Being that has already been exemplified in the hero's life and actions, it does not return to the past. This would be quite impossible, for Dasein's Being is always engaged in concern for the future.[61] This is why it has been so important in the twentieth and twenty-first centuries that some LGBT people have come out of the closet and are visible in the media. By asserting our presence, we challenge opposition to our existence and thus show others that it is possible to live, even thrive, within a community. These others do not live the same life as their predecessors, but they live their own lives within a community that has already been challenged and recognizes them as members whose existence is not a matter of debate. This is merely one example of what is going on during the moments when Dasein is authentically historical: those possibilities for being that are represented by the hero in the past are taken up again by a futurally oriented Dasein. They are varied by each particular Dasein's own situation of Being-in-the-world and Being-with-others, so they are never quite the same. At times, this process is engaged in overcoming oppression, but at others this is the story of how individuals are able to Be what they are, in the everydayness of their particular time and place. Conditions are never ideal; this is why it is so fruitful to talk about Dasein in its facticity, because Dasein is never an abstraction. Dasein is what "is there," what struggles to survive and to clear a space for itself within a complex matrix of frequently competing pressures, drawing on the success of others to conjure its own. The themes repeat but are always varied anew in each Dasein.

Inequality in social relations has the potential, under certain conditions, to bring about the uncanniness necessary for effectuating authenticity. When power discourses painfully fail to adequately speak to some experience, or when they oppress some individuals outright, the conditions created by *das Man* have the potential to force uncanniness on these members of a culture. In such cases, Dasein is thrown forcefully out of its average everydayness and is forced to either strive to conform to the dominant script or create a new script, one that will present a viable challenge to the existing power discourse. In all such cases, a break can be made (or forced) away from fallenness and toward the radical, transgressive individuation that is essential to authenticity. The development of new means of rendering the world and Dasein's place in it intelligible opens up to Dasein its ownmost potentiality-for-Being in a way that responds to the dominant discourses of power and engages them in such a way that quite literally and in a very practical sense "changes the world." When Dasein works, it changes entities within the world, to a greater or lesser degree, but when Dasein *transgresses norms*, it has the potential to reshape the world itself, by means of innovation and transgression, so that the context in which entities, and Dasein itself, are meaningful is understood in a different way. Dr. Martin Luther King Jr. is an example of this; he transgressed law and racial norms. In so doing, he used available discourses to change what race means in the United States. King provides a helpful example for how Dasein navigates its world because his case was so remarkable, but everyday Dasein also reshapes the world by means of innovation and transgression on a smaller scale.

Now, since Dasein interprets itself primarily according to its relation to others, and since gender is cultural classification of Dasein into types, it follows that *Mitsein* is always implicated in and concerned with gender. From this, it then follows that gender is far from being ontologically secondary, something simply "tacked onto" a being that has a gender-neutral basic existence, like Mr. or Mrs. Potato Head. Gender may be a function of *Mitsein*, but it still needs to be seen as equiprimordial with other functions, such as care. Since all possible ways of Being are shaped by the social context in which individuals operate, there are no contexts that dispense with gender. Dasein's identity is always already gendered, and this shapes its potentiality for Being-in-the-world. Thus, there are no possibilities of Being that are gender-free or gender neutral. This brings to mind Beauvoir's famous words: "But if I wish to define myself, I must first of all say: 'I am a woman'; on this truth must be based all further discussion."[62] This is far from being an unusual sentiment, and she was absolutely correct in thinking it needed to be accounted for. But it is also certain that what Beauvoir means by the statement "I am a woman"[63] is something quite different from what a Greek woman of the fourth century

BCE, or an American woman of the twenty-first century, would mean by the same statement. The words may translate literally as the same, but the connotations are quite different, as read within cultural contexts of meaningfulness and discourses of power. Whereas Beauvoir famously demonstrates that biology is not destiny—that is, that "biological sex" is not necessarily the cause of "gender"—it is also the case that gender is not fixed and predetermined by the social context and *das Man*. Some individuals' gender is problematic because they do not meet the cultural expectations they are enjoined by *das Man* to fulfill. If gender were entirely imposed by social context, this could not happen, and there could be no transgender people; everyone would just conform without difficulty. But if gender is, rather, a field of possibility, then it is possible that authentic Dasein might vary existing themes in order to create new modes of intelligibility by which to both understand and dwell in-the-world.

Unequal social conditions create an underlying state of flux within any given culture, however stable and well established that culture may be on the surface. So it goes with gender. It might seem at first glance that gender is entirely dictated by the presuppositions and traditions of *das Man*, yet as generations pass, it is clear that the ways in which types of Dasein are delineated shift and transform themselves, according to the fashion or the needs of cultures as they change. The only constant seems to be that Dasein *is* divided and delineated according to types within the social context. Dasein is indebted to a specific historical culture in all its dealings with the world and others,[64] so, since the being of each Dasein is factical and historical, the theme of gender, too, is subject to both this cultural past and future-oriented variation. While Dasein always already dwells within a world in which gender is a given, it does not follow from this that authentic Dasein is compelled by its history to replay gender in exactly the same form that it has always been played. The shared medium of intelligibility according to which gender is understood is mutable and can be approached anew by authentic Dasein.

Since cultural groups are divided, there is frequently conflict between their divisions. Some factions dominate and oppress others. One of the functions of a dominant faction is that it "constructs social identities for oppressed groups that perpetuates [*sic*] their unequal status."[65] Not only are the myths that the dominant group allows, perpetuates, and promotes suited for maintaining subordination, but they also turn away from alternative understandings of history and limit the possible ways that the shared medium of intelligibility can be meaningful for the subordinated members of the culture. This practice creates a world in which the subordinate members of that culture are "left out in the cold." Privilege ensconces dominant types ever more deeply in their fallen state, and in such a way that they are unaware of their privilege. On the other hand, those whose types are not among the dominant ones of their culture are put in a state of constant unsettledness, or uncanniness, which is the very condition necessary for Dasein to achieve authenticity. It is those whose gender is not in conformity with the expectations of *das Man* who are most likely to broach questions of gender and related issues of social justice, with an authentic mien. For the dominant factions, who are comfortable, the attitudes and presuppositions of *das Man* operate just fine. It is for those who are subordinated or oppressed that the traditional presuppositions regarding gender "break down" and fail to fulfill their function within Dasein's fallen state. Just as a chair tends to go unnoticed as long as it operates correctly but gains attention when it breaks, so it goes with gender. As long as the internal hierarchy of *das Man* operates with accordance to the demands of everyday factical life, it goes unnoticed. But for those who are situated within a social group in such a way that the internal hierarchy of the gender system in *das Man* is an impediment to everyday factical life, the discord can act as a call back from unreflective everydayness into the reticence and resolve of their ownmost potentiality-for-Being.[66]

When this happens, there is a potential—but no guarantee—that Dasein will rethink its presuppositions regarding gender to undertake an applied ontology of itself and of its world. This always happens within a historical context and thus is always a struggle against the heritage that has produced the oppression and subsequent uncanniness among the oppressed. Like the chrysalis, which is so tough that it forces the butterfly to develop the capacity to live in the course of its struggle to emerge, the historical situation of any oppressed Dasein has the capacity to force those who are disenfranchised by their social context to rewrite scripts, to vary themes, and ultimately, to seize possession of their own Being-in-the-world and Being-with-others.

In the end, of course, these authentic stances may in turn become the dominant power discourses that are responsible for oppressing others. Those who lack privilege succeed in overthrowing oppression and then enjoy their own privilege. All they have to do for this to happen is become adopted by *das Man* as exemplars of "just the way it is." If it were possible to attribute anything like a will to *das Man*, it would be the will to maintain and perpetuate the status quo; the comfortable, familiar abode of "how things are done" is maintained by the common sense of any given culture. This is not of necessity a problem; it is precisely what makes a culture operate smoothly. It is a problem only when the system attempts to preclude necessary innovation on the system itself. For the most part, *das Man* rejects the "abnormal," including innovation, which is always a violation of existing norms. Adopting an authentic mien regarding many aspects of cultural presuppositions (including and perhaps especially gender norms) that *das Man* takes for granted amounts to risking the disapprobation of *das Man*, which can take the form of condemnation and even violence. And yet, in spite of this, innovation continues to occur, as Dasein is engaged with the world in terms of its possibility. Innovation is inevitable, since each Dasein engages in its work from an individual orientation in-the-world that is, in each case, its own. While there is a culturally normative aspect to gender, Dasein is no automaton, mindlessly reproducing and reenacting the norms established by *das Man*, but rather an active participant in a culture, community, or group. It follows from this that *das Man* is never merely composed of passive individuals who personify the norms it enforces; rather, these norms are generalizations to begin with, simplifications of what is valued or what Dasein tends to be like. Norms provide the context of intelligibility for each Dasein's unique orientation in-the-world but are themselves perfectly embodied in no particular Dasein. They do change, and when they do, the changes may well be established as new norms, and these new norms themselves provide for new possibilities of Being-in-the-world-with-others. They also provide for new possibilities of transgression in the future, as individuals take up new heroes and participate actively in shaping the potentialities-for-Being that are available to them. This happens by means of repeating and varying existing themes in ways that develop ever-new possibilities for Dasein's understanding of itself. Dasein is, as Heidegger insists, essentially an open-ended question to itself that forever calls forth new answers, never finished or fully established.

NOTES

1. Chanter, "The Problematic Normative Assumptions of Heidegger's Ontology," 76–77.

2. He does say that body is an essential part of what a human being is but does not go on from there. Cf. Heidegger, *Being and Time*, 73; H. 48.

3. Ibid., 74; H. 48.

4. Ibid., 153; H. 117 (emphasis in original).

5. Ibid., 141; H. 107.

6. Ibid., 145–146; H. 110–111. See also ibid., 187; H. 147 and ibid., 95; H. 67.

7. I thank Gayle Salamon for pushing me to answer this important question.

8. Heidegger, *Being and Time*, 444; H. 392.

9. Derrida, "Geschlecht," 54.

10. Martin Heidegger, *The Metaphysical Foundations of Logic*, trans. Michael Heim (Indianapolis: Indiana University Press, 1984), 136 (emphasis in original).

11. Nancy J. Holland, "'The Universe Is Made of Stories, Not of Atoms': Heidegger and the Feminine They-Self," in *Feminist Interpretations of Martin Heidegger*, ed. Nancy J. Holland and Patricia Huntington (University Park: Pennsylvania University Press), 137.

12. Heidegger, *Being and Time*, 237; H. 193. "For the sake of its potentiality-for-Being, any Dasein is as it factically is." 346; H. 299–300. "The Situation is the 'there' which is disclosed in resoluteness—the 'there' as which the existent entity is there. It is not a framework present-at-hand in which Dasein occurs, or into which it might even just bring itself. . . . The current factical involvement-character of the circumstances discloses itself to the Self only when that involvement-character is such that one has resolved upon the 'there' as which that Self, in existing, has to be." 346; H. 299. "Every ontologically explicit question about Dasein's Being has had the way already prepared for it by the kind of Being which Dasein has." 360; H. 312.

13. Holland, "'The Universe Is Made of Stories, Not of Atoms,'" 137.

14. "We have no knowledge of single corporeal things, not because of their particularity, but on account of the matter, which is their principle of individuation. Accordingly, if there be any single things subsisting without matter, as the angels are, there is nothing to prevent them from being actually intelligible." Thomas Aquinas, *Summa Theologica*, trans. Fathers of the English Dominican Province (New York: Benziger Bros., 1947), I.56.1, ad. 2.

15. Heidegger, *The Metaphysical Foundations of Logic*, 136.

16. This priority may or may not be temporal priority. If it is temporal, then we have got something like the traditional preexisting soul. If it is ontologically prior, then we still have a problem, because we are trying to talk about an element of Dasein independently of its facticity.

17. Heidegger, *The Metaphysical Foundations of Logic*, 136–137 (emphasis in original).

18. Heidegger, *Being and Time*, 431; H. 379.

19. Derrida, "Geschlecht," 68.

20. Chanter, "The Problematic Normative Assumptions of Heidegger's Ontology," 98.

21. Heidegger, *Being and Time*, 165; H. 127.

22. Leland, "Conflictual Culture and Authenticity," 106.

23. Heidegger, "The Origin of the Work of Art," 159–161.

24. Edmund Husserl, *Ideas Pertaining to a Pure Phenomenology and to a Phenomenological Philosophy: Second Book, Studies in the Phenomenology of Constitution*, trans. Richard. Rojcewicz and André Schuwer (Boston: Kluwer Academic, 1989), 61 (emphasis in original).

25. Ibid., 65 (emphasis in original).

26. Of course, the fact that Husserl is not talking about ethics does not preclude any ethical determinations being drawn from his account of perception and normality.

27. Husserl, *Ideas: Second Book*, 94.

28. Ibid., 66. At first, this sets off alarm bells, because it implies that any abnormality is inherently contradictory to truth, and this is, again, an ethical matter rather than a phenomenological one.

29. Ibid., 94.

30. Ibid., 64.

31. Maurice Merleau-Ponty, *Phenomenology of Perception*, trans. Colin Smith (New York: Routledge, 1962), 78.

32. Ibid., 184.

33. Ibid., 196.

34. Ibid., 195.

35. Sara Heinämaa, *Toward a Phenomenology of Sexual Difference: Husserl, Merleau-Ponty, Beauvoir* (New York: Rowman and Littlefield, 2003), 67.

36. Merleau-Ponty, *Phenomenology of Perception*, 231.

37. Maurice Merleau-Ponty, *Signs*, trans. Richard C. McCleary (Chicago: Northwestern University Press, 1964), 228 (emphasis in original).

38. Ibid., 54.

39. Merleau-Ponty, *Phenomenology of Perception*, 412.

40. Ibid., 419.

41. Ibid., 510.

42. Ibid., 523.

43. See Jana Sawicki, "Heidegger and Foucault: Escaping Technological Nihilism," in *Foucault and Heidegger: Critical Encounters*, ed. Alan Milchman and Alan Rosenberg (Minneapolis: University of Minnesota Press, 2003), 55–73.

44. See Jana Sawicki, "Identity Politics and Sexual Freedom," in *Disciplining Foucault: Feminism, Power, and the Body* (New York: Routledge, 1991), 33–48.

45. There is a claim made by some that transsexuals do women a disservice by rein-scribing gender norms, rather than challenging them. I have been asked to address this claim, but I opt to do so in a note because I do not want it to receive more attention than it deserves. The argument goes: Feminism seeks to eradicate the harm done by rigid pre-scriptive gender roles. Switching roles, instead of working to broaden what the categories mean or eliminating gender categories altogether, grants legitimacy to the categories as they currently exist and thus legitimates the harm that they do. This argument is an over-simplification of both feminism and of the complex phenomenon that is gender. It also does not accurately address the experience reported by a great many transgender and transsexual individuals.

While gender is a social construction and thus a contingency, it is not the case that it is also a personal choice. (Neither are other social constructions—money is a social construction, yet I cannot choose to be wealthy and have it be so simply because of my choice, however much I might wish to. The only way to transform myself into a wealthy person is to operate within the social construction that is an economic system.) I argue that the very existence of transgender and transsexual individuals stands as a challenge to the current form of gender norms and pushes against them in ways that force their ac-commodation of more types of people.

Furthermore, there do exist those who challenge gender norms without transi-tioning to a gender other than the one they were assigned at birth, such as genderqueer, nonbinary, and agender people. Transgender and transsexual individuals exist in context with other varieties of gender transgressor and cisgender individuals, suborning rigid and unjust understandings of gender by providing a constant resistance.

Finally, it is a mystery to me just *how* anyone can exist in any culture without par-ticipating in the social constructions employed by that culture. Why is it that transgen-der and transsexual individuals seem to be tasked with the responsibility to somehow create, *ex nihilo*, means of existence that are simply not intelligible within the culture in which we dwell? The claims of those who exclude transgender and transsexual pos-sibilities amount to an attempt (doomed to failure) to evict trans people from the field of freedom and intelligibility entirely. The only way to achieve justice for those harmed by prescriptive gender roles is to exert pressure on the discourses that govern gender and thus to change the world.

46. Foucault, "A Preface to Transgression," 71.

47. Ibid., 85.

48. Ibid., 72.

49. Ibid., 73.

50. Foucault, *The History of Sexuality*, 1:43–44.

51. Ibid., 1:101.

52. Ibid.

53. As of this writing, it is becoming clear that the fight for marriage equality has been largely successful. In response to this loss, opponents are now turning their hostility on trans people. Ballot measures seeking to restrict access to public bathrooms are springing up around the United States. I suspect with sadness that the next decade or so will be a fight for the rights of gender transgressive persons, and that significant numbers of gays and lesbians will join with social conservatives in opposition to these rights being extended or recognized.

54. Foucault, *The History of Sexuality*, 1:40–41, 155–156.

55. "Discourses are tactical elements or blocks operating in the field of force relations; there can exist different and even contradictory discourses within the same strategy; they can, on the contrary, circulate without changing their form from one strategy to another, opposing strategy." Ibid., 1:101–102.

56. Beauvoir, *The Second Sex*, 267.

57. *Vorhanden* translates to "present-at-hand," or conspicuous as itself. Things that are *vorhanden* are things that are to be regarded as objects of reflection, instead of as mere tools, used unreflectively, to accomplish some other work.

58. Leland, "Conflictual Culture and Authenticity," 113.

59. Heidegger, *Being and Time*, 436; H. 384.

60. Given Heidegger's political ignominy, it should be noted that the phenomenological conception of the "hero" is not the same thing as the fascist conception of the hero. The former is a descriptive mechanism and the latter an indefensible political commitment. In the fascist conception, as Umberto Eco famously noted, heroism is the norm to which all citizens aspire, the hero "craves heroic death, advertised as the best reward for a heroic life." Umberto Eco, "Ur-Fascism," *New York Review of Books*, June 22, 1995, http://www.nybooks.com/articles/1995/06/22/ur-fascism. The phenomenological hero described in *Being and Time*, on the other hand, is not essentially caught up in a cult of death but is characterized as being a model for living a life. To be sure, the fascist model could be *one* way to understand the phenomenological hero, and Heidegger's own fascism demands acknowledgement of that fact, but the characterization of the hero in *Being and Time* is much more fruitful and need not be limited to the narrower conception of the hero or heroism.

61. Heidegger, *Being and Time*, 437–438; H. 385–386.

62. Beauvoir, *The Second Sex*, xxi.

63. Ibid.

64. Leland, "Conflictual Culture and Authenticity," 115.

65. Ibid., 124.

66. Heidegger, *Being and Time*, 322; H. 277.

CHAPTER 4

GENDER AND INDIVIDUATION

IN FEMINIST AND gender theory, social construction theory is almost universally invoked. The essentialist position (to which the constructionist model is a very strong response) is that there is something essential to femininity, to femaleness, and to women. This stance persists in some feminist theory and certainly endures in the medical field.[1] This essential "something" might be conceived of as being seated in biological difference or, as in Freud, in psychological difference; or it might be taken to be primarily social, yet peculiar to women, as in Irigaray's or Noddings's understandings of mother love and caring.[2] Wherever the locus of the feminine is understood to be in essentialist theory, it is taken to be identifiable and stable, one feature that is common to all who are identifiable as female and feminine and that can act as the basis for a complex of feminist theory, legislation, and social policy. It is certainly the case that feminist thinkers do need to ground their theories in some feature or aspect of human experience by which those whose value is being defended can be identified. In essentialist theory, this takes the form of one definition or another of "the feminine."[3] There is a difficulty, however: nobody has ever identified one feature in which to seat "the feminine" that is universal to all women and exclusive of all men.

The problem here is that essentialist accounts of gender, while working within the tradition, are trying to apply a positive value or definition of the feminine to the existing paradigm, which defines the feminine as that which is a "not," or a flaw. Interestingly, one of the most characteristic physical denotations of femaleness and femininity is the vagina, which is regarded as a hole, literally, a sheath; an absence that is defined by what is not present, the penis.[4] From Sesostris to Irigaray, this synecdoche endures. The feminine is the Other to the positively defined masculine. The masculine here refers to the singular, the unitary, and the universal that serves as a reliable foundation for more of the kind of reasoning that seeks the singular, unitary, and universal answers that account for reality: in short, the Western metaphysical tradition. Subjecthood, within the tradition, is associated with the masculine. The feminine is the plural, the volatile, the specific. The feminine is thus precisely that which cannot be reliably defined or granted subjecthood. And thus in a curious paradox, since femininity is precisely what is excluded by the tradition of exclusive binarism, feminist essentialism seeks to define what is always already indefinable within the tradition in which it is operating. In other words, feminist essentialism, in any of its forms, presupposes some sort of stable identity, a subjectivizing of the feminine into a traditional, immutable substantive subject, which is exactly what femininity is defined as not being. Such a model of human nature inherits all the contradictions of Western metaphysics and the Cartesian subject-object distinction that Heidegger seeks to bypass with the model of Dasein and that I seek here to bypass by employing an applied ontology to examine the intersections of Heidegger, Foucault, and Butler. The presupposition of a stable subject is, as Heidegger notes, "indeed a baleful one, if its ontological necessity and especially its ontological meaning are to be left in the dark."[5] Furthermore, it is the presupposition of an essential feminine-as-lack that lies at the heart of much of the justification for the oppression of women throughout Western history. Women have been denied subjecthood,[6] political significance, and autonomy on the basis of their essentially "feminine natures," and this state of affairs is simply untenable if all instances of Dasein are equally Being-there and equally crucial to the Being-with of others. And it is not only women who suffer from this exclusion but also anyone who transgresses the strict polarity of gender norms, which is to say, everyone, at least from time to time. Nobody is entirely masculine or entirely feminine. Whereas rationality is traditionally a masculine trait, empathy is traditionally seen as feminine. Nobody can be rational without language, however, and language acquisition is only achieved through empathy, wherein multiple people quite literally have the same thought at the same time, conveyed through words or other linguistic media. To achieve masculine rationality, then, each individual must also have mastered feminine empathy to some degree. No woman is purely feminine; nor is any man purely masculine. Such a woman would be an utterly passive being, to the point of being an object. Such a man would be pure narcissistic action—Beowulf on 'roid rage, as it were.

At heart, the traditional model of gender is largely predicated on the relationship of mind and body and the concomitant presupposition of mind-body dualism that regards gender as a consequence of biological sex. The sex-gender distinction is an effect of the radical distinction between mind and body, a historical method of classification, which is exclusionary in character but which also allows for the distinction between the corporeal aspects of human bodies and the relational aspects of human experience. The system is designed to define by means of exclusion of some possibilities for Being that are enacted and embodied in human experience. Only within such a dualistic model can it make any sense to speak of "a man trapped in a woman's body" or vice versa.[7] But such a model results in the definition of some human beings as what they are not (as not-heterosexual, not-cisgender, not-man, not-woman), rather than as what they *are*. In so doing, it enacts, to use Heidegger's terminology, a kind of harmful *Gestell* (enframing) on such people, which excludes their very existence from the sphere of intelligibility.

Gestell, Traditionally Understood

In "Discourse on Thinking," Heidegger distinguishes between calculative thinking and meditative thinking. Calculative thinking enumerates, whereas meditative thinking contemplates. Calculation searches for economy and efficiency, grinding out numbers, statistics, and probabilities without concern for the human meaning of those numbers, statistics, and possibilities.[8] Despite best intentions, calculative thinking affects the type of thoughts someone can have. This kind of thinking is, by its very definition, concerned with specific purposes and definite results; it never takes the "long view" regarding its own activity, even when that activity is beneficent. When relationships with others and with entities in the world are reduced to measurement and classification, there is a concomitant risk of reducing human beings to measurements and classifications. When merged with modern science, calculative thinking becomes technological thinking, because it no longer merely calculates but also produces technological innovations. This kind of thinking leads to what Heidegger calls "enframing" (*Gestell*). The *essence* of technology is not about tools; it is about the tendency to enframe the entities that exist in the world, limiting any conception of them to their usefulness for human beings.[9] When something is allowed to be involved and be significant in only one way, its usefulness, that thing is enframed. It never has the chance to expand beyond present understanding into something new, so enframing can amount to "injurious neglect."[10] This is because in enframing, the "essential unfolding of technology threatens revealing, threatens it with the possibility that all revealing will be consumed in ordering and that everything will present itself only in the unconcealment of standing reserve."[11] Heidegger clearly sees enframing as a threat, and what it threatens is the revealing of the value of human life itself, since it is reduced to "standing reserve," or that which is meaningful only in terms of its usefulness as a means to attaining an end. The twentieth century, marked by peculiarly bureaucratic and economic trends, fosters just such an intentional stance.

In meditative thinking, on the other hand, there is little that is immediately profitable. The value of meditative thinking lies in the questions it raises and the relationships it discloses. When thinking is freed from the expectation that it will satisfy specific purposes and provide definite results, it is possible to "engage ourselves with what at first sight does not go together at all."[12] In other words, meditative thinking is needed to question the significance of the individual choices made in technological thinking, as well as relationships to entities in the world. Individuals are able, by means of meditative thinking, to recognize the pitfalls and the opportunities to which calculative thinking can lead.

Although Heidegger did not address this topic specifically, it is clear that the binary models of sex and gender (male-female and masculine-feminine) are themselves a kind of *Gestell*, and as such run the risk of excluding the possibility that more than two types of sexed and gendered human beings exist at all or can be recognized as existing. The binary classificatory system itself quite literally excludes the possibility of difference, innovation, or change, and within it human beings run the risk of becoming nothing more than a standing reserve that exists to reflect the system, rather than the system existing to reflect and benefit human beings. The lack of visibility or discussion of those who transgress traditional gender paradigms is the result of one kind of *Gestell*—if there are no words for such people, then there is no way to discuss the possibility of their existence. But the definition of such people as a lack, as what they are not, is another kind of *Gestell*.[13] This move parallels Aristotle's designation of women as being on a lower level than men in an ontological hierarchy in that it defines the gender transgressive individual as an inverted or damaged version of an ideally sexed human being. The language of mind-body dualism, which is the foundational method that is repeated in the production of sex and gender binaries, always already prejudges the gender transgressive individual by placing such an individual into a subordinate position by naming it *as a lack of* genuine Being. Individuals come to understand themselves as individuals in relation to measured norms, which are established by binary models:

> Norms homogenize the group by enabling all differences among its members to be understood as deviations from a norm and therefore essentially related to it. No one stands outside the normalization. . . . There is no pure difference, only measurable difference. At the same time, norms individualize each member of the group by enabling a precise characterization of that person . . . as a case history of particular, measurable degrees of deviation from the set of norms.[14]

Yet this is a paradox: what is normal is defined by contrast with deviation from the norm, and what is known to be is only intelligible because of a contrast with the possibility for it not to be. That is, the only way of defining the typical within a dualistic model is by acknowledging the possibility of the existence of the atypical, and it is that which falls outside the range of the typical that discloses the limits of the typical. Paradoxically, a dualistic methodology ends up simultaneously excluding the possibility of transgressive individuals' existence and relying on our existence to define and name the typical.

Clearly, another model of human experience is possible, one that accounts for factical and historical experience and allows each case of Dasein to be disclosed as what it is, not merely in terms of what it is not or in relation to norms. In its facticity, Dasein is not easily defined, since is not a stable substance that can be classified once and for all and expected to stay that way. Dasein is contingent, contextual, factical, and historical—in short, messy. Beauvoir's critique of Western ethics—namely, that it attempts to create systems that are universal and that consequently efface the plurality and contingency of concrete human beings—can also be leveled against most theories and paradigms regarding gender.[15] *Das Man*'s insistence that every Dasein fit tidily into a binary system that defines its very manner of being-in-the-world runs the risk of becoming fanaticism, suborning the good of human beings to the value of an object. As Beauvoir describes it,

> It is the fanaticism of the Inquisition which does not hesitate to impose a credo, that is, an internal movement, by means of external constraints. It is the fanaticism of the Vigilantes of America who defend morality by means of lynchings. It is the political fanaticism which empties politics of all human content and imposes the State, not *for* individuals, but *against* them.[16]

It is this fanaticism that in February 2008 led a schoolchild to shoot a classmate for the "crime" of gender transgression and to justify this murder by blaming it on the victim and on those who tolerated the victim's transgression.[17] It is this fanaticism that led a family to so thoroughly isolate a transgender daughter that she took her own life in despair.[18] *Das Man* is composed of multiple individuals, all of whom are concrete, and yet imposes its will to conformity on each, citing the normal as a universal value at which each ought to aim. In *das Man*, the normal is normativized into an ethical injunction. If this will to conformity is bolstered with preconceptions that efface the diversity of many particular orientations in-the-world, violent fanaticism can result. If justice is to be done and the rendering of Dasein into a mere statistic, caricature, or type is to be avoided, a model that accounts for the intrinsic messiness of Dasein and the perpetual tension that obtains between individuated Dasein and *das Man* is required. Butler's account of gender and identity sows the seed of just such a model.

Judith Butler's Challenge of Coherent Identity

In "Phantasmatic Identification and the Assumption of Sex," Butler questions political and social insistence on coherent identities in general, and in "Bodies That Matter," she asks why this insistence seems to regard the biological as the irreducible point of coherence on which identities are built. The second question is aimed at biological essentialism, whereas the first is a challenge to the traditional notion of the coherent subject:

> The insistence on coherent identity as a point of departure presumes that what a "subject" is is already known, already fixed, and that that ready-made subject might enter the world to renegotiate its place. But if that very subject produces its coherence at the cost of its own complexity, the crossings of identifications of which it is itself composed, then that subject forecloses the kinds of contestatory connections that might democratize the field of its own operation.[19]

But where does this coherent subject come from? It can only come from identification with certain characteristics and repudiation of others. But nothing can be identified with or repudiated except by a subject. Butler reveals a circularity here: we cannot have x until we have y, and we cannot have y until we have x. The insistence on coherent subjects requires that the subject abase that which it "is not," through repudiation. But identifying the self by means of repudiation necessitates that identity be reliant on the very thing that is repudiated, as is shown by the curious twist that allowed the homosexual to exist before the heterosexual. This is precisely what Butler accomplishes by positing her performative model of gender; the circle described above does not entail logical contradiction if the presupposition that human identity takes the form of a fixed, coherent subject is rejected. The performative model leaves room for the subject to retain its complexity and plural identifications, while also maintaining its integrity as a subject that performs these identities, even when he or she falls prey to the all too common human foible of being inconsistent.

But then, what is a self? What makes me *me* and not, rather, someone else? What would this discussion of gender look like without the presumption of a coherent subject? How would this strategy change the discursive landscape? Well, it looks a lot like a discussion of Dasein; Heidegger has already laid the foundation for this approach. As far as the challenge to the philosophical tradition's investment in the coherent subject goes, Butler's and Heidegger's questions and models of human Being resonate with one another, like parts sung in a choral work. Recalling that Dasein is a way to resist defining the self as a thing or entity while retaining a means of examining lived experience brings the connections between these thinkers into clarity. Dasein is its embodied facticity revealed in the stories it tells. Furthermore, Dasein is always already thrown in a world shaped by *das Man*, invested in conformity to the public self. Heidegger offers an account of conformity and of individual breaks with fallenness into authenticity, but he never addresses alterity within the social body. Butler picks up these themes and adds a harmonizing examination of difference to Heidegger's groundwork, particularly with regard to gender differences, and how this difference is played out in the social sphere, including ethical and political theory. This addition of difference is no trivial variation; it has the potential to yield insight into the ways Dasein is gendered and also into other ways that *das Man* is invested in similarity. The enforcement of similarity by means of the establishment of gender norms is significant to everyone's Being, not merely to the Being of gender transgressors, because every Dasein is always already gendered. This is where Heidegger's and Butler's theories converge, and the benefit of a cooperative and interrelational methodology that employs both theories in undertaking an applied ontology of gender emerges.

According to Butler, gender, like the subject generally, is a complexity, never a whole, and never fully given. It is an experienced phenomenon, not a set of prescriptive definitions. Gender is contingent on context, culture, and situatedness—in short, on innumerable specific, factical assemblages and regulatory practices of gender that govern identity.[20] This may look surprising, but it is almost exactly a description of the differentiated but still fallen Dasein that is found in Heidegger's *Being and Time*. The institution of gender is a descriptive, hermeneutic circle in the Heideggerian sense: *Das Man* institutes norms of gender, which are then formative of Dasein's possibility, and which Dasein may or may not use or challenge in its being called to authenticity.[21] In turn, Dasein *performs* its gender and perpetuates the institution, for even challenge is a recognition of the institution. This does not mean that gender remains static. There is a good deal of change going on in the realm of gender, but that change is sometimes brought about by those who transgress *das Man*'s institution of gender and then incorporate it into the institution itself. As Butler puts it, "Gender is the repeated stylization of the body, a set of repeated acts within a highly rigid regulatory frame that congeal over time to produce the appearance of substance, of a natural sort of being."[22] Claims made by *das Man* that gender norms are what they are because they represent some kind of universal truth of human Being are actually founded in the norms that *das Man* institutes, perpetuates, and enforces.

Gender, then, is understood in Butler's thinking as a social construction characterized by a specific kind of performativity: "not a singular or deliberative 'act,' but rather, as the reiterative and citational practice by which discourse produces the effects that it names."[23] Performativity is a matter of the way an individual, a society, a community, a language group, a culture, and so on embody, repeat, and live out beliefs and presuppositions about things. "Discourse," according to Butler, is composed of "complex and convergent chains in which 'effects' are vectors of power. . . . [T]he power of discourse [is able] to circumscribe the domain of intelligibility."[24] Through discourse, the possible, what is intelligible within the matrix of the discourse itself, is named. Through performance, what has been named in discourse is brought about. So gender is performative in that discourse names what is masculine and what is feminine (English has no other option for referring to persons, although some languages include a neuter, such as *das Kind* in German), and Dasein, in being masculine or feminine, embodies this naming in performativity. This, too, is consonant with Heidegger's understanding of *das Man*. What is named in discourse is not merely particular acts by particular humans but rather what *das Man* thinks is appropriate or correct about the world. "They" say that women who shave their legs are more attractive to men, for instance, so individual women shave their legs, thus embodying the discourse about leg shaving. Should an individual woman decide not to shave, she does not change the discourse, but she does run the danger of being abjected by it. Why is leg shaving feminine? Because *das Man* says it is. Why does *das Man* regard shaving as feminine? Because women do it. Why do women shave their legs? Because *das Man* tells them to and punishes them for not shaving. Those who perform gender in the ways ratified by the dominant discourse fall within the norm. They are recognized as subjects and are privileged in social interactions because they are "as they should be." Those who fall outside the norm are abjected.[25] Their subjecthood, their very humanity, is in question precisely because they fall outside of the discourse that names what the human is. Leg shaving is an example with relatively low stakes, yet it is indicative of how abjection operates. Many women both hate shaving their legs and are appalled at the notion of stopping. *Das Man*'s commitment to maintaining gender norms extends all the more strongly to such high-stakes issues as employment, medical care, sexual freedom, and education, exerting a very real pressure on women to remain "in their place."

In discussing Butler, it is important to note that saying a phenomenon is constructed does not claim that any individual has complete freedom regarding that construction. It is not a matter of forming the world and oneself as one pleases, a make-believe or adornment.[26] This is a common error made by critics of social construction theory. To say that gender is a social construction is not to say that each individual has absolute choice regarding his or her gender. Rather, it is to say that any given culture's understanding of gender is the site of what is and what is not possible within that culture. Gender manifests itself differently in different cultural discourses, but it is always there. Furthermore, nothing can be spoken of unless it is defined. The definitions of things are their limitations, what they exclude. These limitations are what make a thing what it is, as the imaginary line drawn across the land is what makes Canada and the United States what they are. While cultures define gender, by means of the performance of gender, they do not determine it fully in advance. That is, the laws of gender and sexual difference are not the same as the laws of logic. (Quite a lot of the time, they are not even logical.) It is always the case that the law of noncontradiction holds, by definition. It is not always the case that a particular kind of action is masculine or feminine. That is contingent on culture and era. The repetition of acts is essential to performativity, and "a performative functions to produce that which it declares."[27] What does it declare and produce? Nothing other than norms. Norms do change over time, but they are always there in one form or another and are always invoked. The law that enjoins adherence to norms "works only by reworking a set of already operative conventions. And these conventions are grounded in no other legitimating authority than the echo-chain of their own reinvocation."[28] So pressures that enforce heteronormativity function only as a way of reworking and maintaining that which already is: heteronormative values and assumptions. Historically speaking, these pressures do change as the needs of a society

change. Those performatives that are no longer useful or desirable for one reason or another fall by the wayside as social constructions evolve. Blasphemy is
not punished in Western courts, for instance, and Whites Only signs have dis-
appeared from the doorways of emergency rooms. The laws and customs gov-
erning gender function in the same way. Now, the United States has universal
suffrage, women maintain careers, and, as of this writing, marriage equality is
guaranteed by the Supreme Court. In response to these deployments of power
and their concomitant reestablishment of norms, movements to restrict reproductive choice, a resurgence of religiously based homeschooling, and the
introduction of "religious freedom" bills and "bathroom bills" that legitimate
discrimination in state laws have arisen. These responses deploy power that
deliberately clashes with norms, which also shapes the world that Dasein navigates. There can be no blueprint for how all this operates because as the tides
of the social order shift and accommodate various needs, different values arise
and motivate subsequent shifts and vicissitudes, which are themselves later
shifted according to another rubric. Dasein is neither powerless, drawn along
the tide of its world, nor all-powerful and capable of creating ideal choices *ex
nihilo*. Dasein, thrown into its world, does the best it can with what it has.

What is at stake here extends beyond how justice is to be done to those
abjected members of a community whose very existence is threatened by a
discourse that defines them as Other or as outside the realm of concern. It
is also, and more fundamentally, how the discursively unintelligible can be
rendered intelligible. What happens when what is excluded comes to resemble
that which is included, in response to the appearance of something even more
unintelligible? Consider Butler's example of homosexuality as being excluded
by heteronormativity: the stereotypical gender expressions for homosexuals—
"bull dykes" and "queens"—are shaped by heterosexual discourse. By the
very act of proscribing gender violations, custom and law recognize them and
bring them into the sphere of possibility, even if only as those that are forbid-
den. The custom and law that punish homosexuality as a failure to perform
gender in culturally sanctioned ways also create the discursive intelligibility of
those performances. It was necessary for Oscar Wilde's prosecutors to speak
the name of the vice that dare not speak its name in order to prosecute him.
There are no laws or customs against that which is not done, and when an act,
a habit, or a performance is proscribed by law, it is recognized as something
that is possible. In being a recognized as a possibility, transgression becomes
intelligible.

Heterosexuality is recognized precisely because homosexuality is excluded. But what happens when something less familiar to *das Man* than

homosexuality appears on the scene and begins to challenge the discursive intelligibility of both homosexuality and heterosexuality? The general public's response to learning about transgender individuals fits the bill quite well here, since in cases of transgender persons, sexuality is not the central issue; rather, gender identity is. In the United States, homosexuality has become more visible in recent decades, but the common understanding of the gender binary has remained comparatively stable. Certainly, gender norms have shifted, but the two-sex, two-gender model is still generally presupposed. So the phenomenon of transgender individuals presents a challenge to *das Man* to once more confront the issue of intelligibility among its members, as the concept of gender is more clearly divorced from those of "biological sex" and "sexual orientation." Gender norms have always been transgressed by transgender persons, even those who are relatively unambiguously masculine or feminine, simply because a crossing of socially established gender boundaries has occurred. Such a challenge to the discursive norm makes homosexuality appear less disruptive and more intelligible within the bounds of societal expectations by comparison. It seems that the arrival of a phenomenon that draws similarities between that which is excluded and that which is included has the capacity to cause the inclusion of that which was formerly excluded, although this does not necessarily result in the *acceptance* of the formerly excluded phenomenon. A new Other is created, which results in the conceptual alliance of two formerly mutually exclusive phenomena. Cisgender gay people seem relatively normal to most cisgender heterosexual people once they meet someone who is transgender. This does not guarantee greater acceptance of gay people, but it does make possible an alliance of cisgender gay people and cisgender straight people in reinforcing gender norms and opposing trans rights and freedoms. This raises some very interesting questions indeed with regard to the legislative system of the United States, such as what legal sex a transgender person is classified as being and what standards various states use as defining criteria of legal sex, but at the present time such criteria are still almost entirely governed by the medical community, and gender transgression is almost universally pathologized. There is even some dispute in some lesbian and gay communities, and also in feminist communities, about whether transgender persons ought to be included among their numbers.[29] This process of realigning the boundaries between intelligibility and abjection runs the risk of creating what some would call a hierarchy of suffering, wherein some abjected persons are regarded as more deserving of social approbation than others, with the less deserving rendered vulnerable to dehumanization and violence. I do not by any means advocate adopting such a hierarchy of suffering, but at the same time,

I find that this tendency highlights the mutability of the ways that boundaries are drawn and how they apply to everybody, not only to gender transgressive Dasein.

Butler, echoing Heidegger's critique of biologism,[30] notes that essentialism has a tendency to appeal to biology, to the material aspect of the body, and, in "Bodies That Matter," she asks why this is the case.[31] This is an especially salient question in light of the constructed character of how both bodies and gender are understood. Since what is meant by the materiality of women's bodies is contingent on the discourse that has excluded women since at least Plato's time, what can be said about female or feminine materiality is caught up in a discourse that excludes it. This does seem to be pretty shaky ground on which to build a theory of feminism, or of gender, since it provides no positive terms with which to articulate a robust theory of gender. In fact, it amounts to building a theory of coherent identity on precisely that which has been rendered incoherent, unidentifiable, and Other by discourse. Exploring the relation of identity to gender, however, while also *not* presupposing that identity is fixed, stable, or substantive, can free the exploration of gender from the constraints of both naïve biological reductionism and the necessity of defining what is sought prior to the search (which is logically circular). This allows the meaningfulness of the phenomenon of gender to factical life to emerge from the inquiry, placing the priority squarely on Being-in-the-world.

If, as Butler asserts, gender is contingent on context, culture, and situatedness—in short, on a complex intersection of specific, factical assemblages— then a *descriptive* account of the way two phenomena shape and inform one another is possible. Regulatory practices of gender govern identity. They are exercised and enforced by *das Man* and are formative of Dasein's possibility of Being in that they form the factical and existentiell possibilities that are Dasein's Being. Regulating practices create the field of potential. In turn, Dasein performs gender in the ways that are rendered intelligible by *das Man*'s institution of gender, and its performance perpetuates the institution. Of course, each performance is new within its own context, and therefore variations on the themes of gender occur and are incorporated into the institution; in the repetition of themes, gender, as it is understood by *das Man*, gains credence. Dasein expects this sort of repetition. Indeed, repetition and the expectation of repetition are the way that Dasein, which is futurally oriented, makes sense of its life. On this point, Heidegger and Butler are in agreement. Heidegger points out, "By repetition, Dasein first has its own history made manifest,"[32] and Butler writes, "Gender is an identity tenuously constructed in time, instituted in an exterior space through a *stylized repetition of acts*."[33]

Repetition, then, does not prove the universal truth of *das Man*'s conception of gender norms in any objective sense, but it does have the effect of providing the *Gestell*, the framework, according to which Dasein understands itself. Repetition establishes and reestablishes these norms as the context in which truth is evaluated, creating the illusion of nature or necessity, and therefore the enforcement of these norms is crucial to the perpetuation of *das Man* and thus Dasein's understanding of itself. The illusion of nature or necessity in turn influences the way intelligibility is established. For instance, devotion to offspring in some nonhuman species is sometimes cited as "proof" in popular discourses that the role of the female is motherhood, whereas those species in which the female is not the primary caregiver to offspring, intergenerational competition, and evolutionary traits unique to humans are simply disregarded in a blatant case of confirmation bias.[34] In actual fact, motherhood in nonhuman animals takes on none of the ethical dimension it does in humans. The illusion of necessity is perpetuated by the selection of examples that support the story popularly told of motherhood, not the objective facts of motherhood.

Butler also speaks of the operation of "a regulatory practice that seeks to render gender identity uniform throughout a compulsory heterosexuality."[35] This is puzzling. It sounds as though she were making a substance out of culture itself or, in the language of Heidegger, attributing a will to *das Man*, which would raise some real problems with consistency. I do not think that Butler's theory needs to be taken to this extreme, however. It is the case that in most of its historical situations, Western culture has enforced a "compulsory heterosexuality," but can any culture legitimately be said to have a will or any kind of capacity to enforce any kind of compulsory anything? Perhaps, but only in a weak, negative sense of a will to resistance regarding change, not in a strong, positive sense of capacity for choice. It is not too difficult to see how this is done, if Heidegger's terminology may be borrowed again to illustrate: for the most part, *das Man* rejects what is "abnormal" as being uncanny and causing discomfort. Laws are made against many forms of abnormality, but for most of fallen Dasein's activity, no laws are even needed, only "common sense." People tend to dress as others do, to speak in the slang of their place and time, to stand in line and wait their turn. Women hold their knees together when sitting, while men take up more room. The penalty of failing to adhere to the norm is the general disapprobation of *das Man*, an event that, in itself, makes most feel uneasy, if not anxious. In this limited sense, *das Man* "wills" the perpetuation of the status quo by rewarding its repetition. The comfortable, familiar abode of "how things are done" is maintained by the common sense of the culture in which any individual lives. For the most part, this is not a problem. The common sense that determines what is or is not proper makes being-with-others operate smoothly. The problem with this is that such resistance to innovation does not allow for change or growth. Those who risk the condemnation of *das Man* to strike out on their own are the ones who are on the way to authenticity. In a very real sense, those who challenge gender norms transgress the common sense of *das Man* when they strike out in a new direction. Those whose innovations are adopted, however, are the pioneers of change within *das Man*. So *das Man* can be understood as a power that enforces the status quo but not in any conscious sense, and certainly not as a substantive being. Rather, transgression is also a part of the constitution of the power that *das Man* wields, which means that culture need not be understood as being a substance, even when it employs regulatory practices.

Another way that gender norms are challenged and transgressed, as Butler famously points out, is through parody. When predominant heterosexual constructs are played out in a nonheterosexual context, such as drag performances, the artificiality of such constructs becomes plain.[36] To those for whom the compulsory heterosexuality of *das Man* breaks down, heterosexuality and the binary gender system are anything but universal, and when their nonuniversality is established, a clearing is opened up in which other paradigms for understanding and performing gender become possibilities. This is why drag shows can be so much fun: they surprise us with the contingency and illogic of assumptions regarding gender.[37] If the common sense of *das Man* is shown to be contingent regarding biological sex and gender performance, then for those who do not conform to the norm, a new set of possibilities for authentic Being can open itself. Such individuals need not continue to try to operate in a world that is, for them, a kind of breakdown wherein they cannot succeed because their particular ways of Being-in-the-world do not match the social expectations of *das Man*. They can "buck the system," as it were, and seek authenticity by challenging the ordinary, fallen assumptions made by the they-self.

All this confirms Butler's position that "there need not be a 'doer behind the deed,' but that the 'doer' is variably constructed in and through the deed."[38] This resonates nicely with Heidegger's critique of the traditional metaphysical subject, that "*fanciful idealization*"[39] that has made such a confusion of metaphysics throughout Western history. The conception of identity and gender as performative, in breaking down the radical distinction between Dasein and its world, allows the avoidance of the subject-object distinction as well as all the problems it entails and examines the kind of Being that Dasein lives.

Orientation, Individuation, Authenticity

Butler did not see herself as doing ontology of any sort in *Gender Trouble*, and I believe this may have had to do with her commitment to issues of applied ethics and politics:

> There is no ontology of gender on which we might construct a politics, for gender ontologies always operate within established political contexts as normative injunctions, determining what qualifies as intelligible sex, invoking and consolidating the reproductive constraints on sexuality, setting the prescriptive requirements whereby sexed or gendered bodies come into cultural intelligibility. Ontology is, thus, not a foundation, but a normative injunction that operates insidiously by installing itself into political discourse as its necessary ground.[40]

The claim here is in its logical structure, not unlike the one in chapter 2, that political concerns such as family structure have influenced the expectations science has regarding the sex binary. Butler's claim, however, is that *ontologies* are influenced by political concerns and thus serve to reinscribe existing gender norms. My response is that this is true, ontologies are always undertaken within some context of intelligibility, and certainly *regional* ontologies of gender are subject to serving as normative injunctions. But it does not preclude an ontology of gender that elucidates and challenges political concerns. An *applied* ontology, one that deconstructs not only the classificatory systems that govern sex and gender but also the political concerns that have given rise to these classificatory systems, suits very well. Butler demonstrates that gender is a reiterative inscription of regulatory norms and practices, and she does address the issue of how these norms and practices are challenged by transgression. What she does not address, however, is the significance of these norms and practices to human Being in a foundational, ontological sense. A robust account of the phenomenon of gender must not only challenge the coherent subject and investigate how gender is performed by means of reiterative and parodic acts but must also investigate the experiences and classificatory systems that motivate these actions. Furthermore, if these experiences and classificatory systems are to be understood, how they contribute to establishing investment in understanding oneself must also be investigated. Dasein tells its stories and investigates its world—these stories and investigations are precisely what shape Dasein's manner of living out its own Being. This is why there is gender: one of the ways Dasein makes sense of itself and its world is by means of gender.

Butler rejects the claim that gender is a personal choice in *Bodies That Matter*, and I agree with this position.[41] There is certainly normativity involved with cultural inscriptions of gender, and there is also a great deal of variation within these cultural inscriptions, however regulatory they may be. The cultural dictates of gender seem, in some cases, to have unexpected consequences when brought to bear against some. There are individuals who cannot or do not, for whatever reason, perform gender in the expected manners. Such transgressions have been noted, for example, in small children too young to make choices regarding gender. In such cases, the most urgent questions concern the child's well-being. Secondary questions include: What is going on with gender transgressive types of Dasein? If the relationship between gender and biological sex is contingent, how far does the contingency go? How do we account for the experience that some have in feeling compelled to perform a gender that they were not assigned at birth? The scientific answer to the question of what causes gender transgression is unknown, but some insight into the way the phenomena of transgression are experienced by Dasein is available. It appears that there is something inherent, singular, and unique about some individual (and perhaps all) situatedness and experience that is felt as a compulsion or at least an inclination to perform gender in a given way. For some, this something does not fit the expectations of *das Man* and compels a challenge to cultural dictates. Butler is correct; this something is not a matter of mere choice, as evidenced by the fact that such individuals frequently try very strenuously indeed to conform and yet suffer grievously for failing to conform successfully. Choosing does not work. (I myself *chose* to be a straight, cisgender woman. It did not do any good. My gender remained intractably of the type that my culture defines as masculine.) But this state of affairs also presents a question that must be asked of the performative model of gender, as it might seem to revert back to a theory that there is some kind of coherent identity at work, which asserts itself in the face of the culture's script:

- If Dasein is entirely Being-in-the-world-with-others, how can any account of abnormality, not only gender nonconformity, be given?
- If gender is not inherent to the person in some way, how is it that everybody does not just conform without difficulty?
- Why does the constructionist model not render this impossible, since it seems to provide the only possibility for rendering human experience intelligible?

According to Heidegger, there is the "moment of vision" that calls Dasein to authenticity, but how could such a moment occur when an individual Dasein understands its very identity differently from the ways acknowledged as possible?

The answer lies in the fact that Dasein does not create, *ex nihilo*, new ways of Being but rather varies the theme of what is presented as possible within a given culture by *das Man*. The most inventive of individuals accomplish their invention within a context of meaningfulness in which they always already dwell, so the constructionist model does not preclude innovation. The dominant perspective still inheres as the seed of any invention. So, too, with gender nonconformity: the most feminine man behaves in a manner that is understood as feminine by his culture, and the most masculine woman behaves in a manner that *das Man* deems masculine. In some, then, it would seem that the moment of vision leads to a variation on the theme of gender normativity, in much the same way as musical innovation plays on the theme of what is already taken for granted in the music world. If these individuals are to make sense of their own Being, they must answer the "call of conscience" in one way or another. They must become "guilty" in the Heideggerian sense of being defined "by a 'not'"[42]—in this case, a "not normal," according to the common sense of *das Man* and its expectations of gender performance. Since being not normal is a transgression of what is expected by *das Man*, such a Dasein is subjected to conditions that impose the uncanniness necessary to achieving authenticity. Suffering occurs.

The question most commonly asked is *why* some variations on the theme of gender cross cultural boundaries and why other variations do not. This way of asking the question places focus on the phenomenon of difference itself, supposing a norm and then examining the instances wherein it is transgressed. This is how the medical and psychiatric communities, which have a tendency to pathologize the atypical, ask the question of gender. There is another way to look at the question of gender, however. If the question is, instead, about the *how* of gender transgression, then the question is about the details of the experience some undergo in such transgression. If focus shifts away from the individual for a moment and moves to *das Man* as a whole, what is to be found but an entity that is composed of individuals who are all always already in the process of individuating, in exuberantly intersecting all the facets of lived experience. It stands to reason that with all this individuating and innovation of unique, factical, and historical individuals going on, some must, by definition, individuate in ways that are not typical of *das Man* as a whole. Cultural norms are dynamic phenomena and individuals are dynamic instances of individuation. Both are always in flux, exerting power on one another. Moreover, as shown above, norms are defined by that which transgresses them. Thus, since Dasein is an exceedingly complex being and cultural norms are exceedingly complex phenomena, it follows that the degree of innovation and variation that can and does occur necessarily entails transgression on the part of some. Norms demand transgression. When looked at from this perspective, the question of *why* some transgress might well be replaced by a sense of wonder that more do not transgress gender norms in radical ways. This is because while transgressive types of Dasein are atypical *as* individuals, it is at the same time necessary that *das Man* include atypical types of Dasein if norms are to exist. To address the question of *how* gender norms are experienced by Dasein, the mechanics of the process of individuation must be examined.

It is in anxiety that Dasein is individuated.[43] For the most part, Dasein flees anxiety and remains in the comfortable familiarity of *das Man*. However, it is also the case that since Dasein is always a specific, historical Dasein, its orientation in the world will always be a specific and particular orientation.[44] Thus, Dasein's very Being is a peculiar tension between its individuated Being and the more public, comfortable Being of its fallen state. This tension demands resoluteness in the face of guilt, which is understood in the Heideggerian sense as responsibility for a lack that is outside Dasein's control. When Dasein experiences uncanniness that disrupts its comfortable fallenness in the world, it no longer has the resources to remain fallen. In such a case, Dasein must resolutely take responsibility for its own Being: it must step out of its concern with the present and retrieve potential responses (memories, stories of what might work) from its past in order to make authentic decisions about its future and the way it will live its life within a given situation that can only ever be partly within its control. Only in resoluteness can Dasein take responsibility for the fact that whatever choice it makes, other options will be excluded. For example, an individual born with ambiguous genitalia does not by any means choose to be born intersex. The atypical body of such a person is the situation in which she finds herself. But such an individual does, as a general rule, find herself to be outside the norm and thus in a state of anxious uncanniness caused either by her own discomfort with her body or by her being the cause of others' anxiety. What this individual *chooses to do about* her intersex condition requires a certain stance of responsibility for a largely uncontrollable situation. This stance is what Heidegger calls the "moment of vision," which involves taking responsibility for directing the course her life will take in response to this situation. When the intersex individual understands her situation, she must answer the call of conscience, projecting her options (i.e., for or against surgery or for adjusting her way of living) on her future and making a choice, which amounts to examining the options available in the situation in which she finds herself and living with that choice. The choices she makes are thus authentic ones. Situations are often not chosen; what is done about them may be. The choices available are the field of freedom.

It is out of this tension between fallenness and individuation that gender transgression arises for some, as a response to Heideggerian guilt and the moment of vision. Some are simply thrown in the world in such a way that how they act is classified as a gender performed in ways not expected by *das Man*, for whatever reason and for which there is no definitive explanation. Since the categories *das Man* uses to classify are always more limited than the potentialities of countless factical experiences, and since they cannot tidily cover all the possible permutations of Being that are actually *lived*, the stage is set for transgressive types of Dasein to arise out of the innate tension that obtains between individual cases of Dasein and *das Man*. One need not resort to theories of essential identity or innateness but only commit to the notion that each instance of Dasein, being factical and historical, has a unique approach, particular to its own perspective, to its own Being-in-the-world. As Heidegger says, in a rare moment of beautiful writing, "The pure 'that it is' shows itself, but the 'whence' and the 'whither' remain in darkness."[45] Individual character may, in some, entail something that does not "fit" gender norms and inclines one toward transgression of the cultural norms according to which one is defined.

Various orientations may be accounted for by the intersectional state of Dasein's thrownness and facticity within even the most heterogeneous community. Dasein's socioeconomic status, race, religious background (or lack thereof), physical abilities and disabilities, biological sex, gender, and even language, to name but a few factors, all contribute to Dasein's orientation in the world. The particular and contingent circumstances and exigencies of Dasein's Being-in-the-world-with-others have their effect on *how* any given Dasein *is* in its world. Being born and raised Catholic does not mean that Dasein will remain Catholic, but it will make Catholicism an important element of that Dasein's life, as something to be embraced, eschewed, tolerated, or changed. But no Dasein is simply "Catholic." Dasein is Catholic and rich, Catholic and poor, Catholic and African American, Catholic and Uruguayan, seventeenth-century Catholic, twenty-first century Catholic, Catholic and sitting on this side of the room, Catholic and sitting on that side of the room, and so on. The ways that Dasein's Being is affected by its particular thrown orientation in the world are innumerable, and the potential complications afforded by all these possibilities are so complex as to render each particular orientation unique, especially as it changes throughout each Dasein's lifetime. Most of the time, such orientations are inauthentically lived as part of Dasein's fallen state, but there is no reason why they must necessarily be either inauthentic or authentic. They are, rather, the necessary condition of authenticity or inauthenticity. Dasein's individual orientation is either that which it accepts and conforms to without much reflection or that to which it creatively and transgressively responds with authentic resoluteness.

Given the complex ways in which Dasein is always already an individual in the world, it is no surprise that its individuation yields differing goals and desires, including those regarding gender and sexuality. As specific modes of Dasein's Being and concern with others, desires are directed toward the potentialities that Dasein seeks to fulfill in its work in the world, and desire itself is the motivator for Dasein's engagement in the in-order-to structure of its Being. What is lacking and what is abundant in each Dasein's Being-in-the-world will differ from one Dasein to another. Given that each Dasein's history and factical situation is unique, it follows that different individuals will exhibit different desires. All of Dasein's undertakings are futurally oriented, and the goals sought are what Dasein, for whatever reasons, desires.

It is clear, then, that differences in orientation are always already present within *das Man* and that each Dasein finds itself uniquely oriented in the world, whether such orientations are or are not caused by biological factors. Medical science may yet discover the biological basis for sexual orientations and gender identities, but whether such a basis is ever found or not, they always already matter and shape lives as social constructions. Does it really make that much difference to experience whether homosexuality or transgender identity has a biological or social cause? At heart, such phenomena are disclosive of Dasein's potentiality for Being-in-the-world and have the capacity to push the limits of the existing "framework" of any understanding of what Dasein is and can be, whatever their causes may be. These phenomena do not necessarily eliminate *Gestell*, the tendency Dasein has of enframing and enclosing phenomena into a fixed, useful model. But *Gestell* is a double-edged sword: it runs the risk of limiting understanding of Dasein's Being to artificially limited potentialities, but it also has the capacity of creating new ways of understanding Dasein's Being by operating as the structure on which new ideas are innovated. It should not be forgotten that *Gestell* means "framework" as well as "limitation" and that a framework, along with its exclusionary limit, is always a basis on which something, be it an office building or a concept such as gender, is built.

Generally, a conceptual model is discarded or expanded on when it ceases to succeed, when it challenges Dasein's capacity to make use of it as a given, when it becomes conspicuous as that which does not suffice to describe Dasein's Being without critical reflection. Such phenomena as atypical sexual or gender orientations have the potential to expand on the framework of how Dasein's Being is understood. These expansions can create *new* frameworks for both calculative/technological and meditative thinking about Dasein's Being that work by rendering experience intelligible and livable. The way in which Dasein expands the framework of its understanding is by repetition. Each Dasein takes up anew the themes provided by *das Man* and varies them according to its particular orientation within its historical situation. When these themes are varied in ways that are not merely world-changing but also norm-changing, they are no longer simply innovative but are also transgressive and create the possibility of new horizons of meaningfulness to appear in Dasein's Being.

Over and against *das Man*'s enforcement of gender norms, then, there is the simple underlying fact that *das Man* is not homogeneous; it is composed of different types of Dasein and of individuals who are all exuberantly, differently oriented in the world. There are not only various ways of dividing types but also individual orientations, perspectives, and goals of each individual. Dasein is dynamic, involved with its own history and future goals, and in its work, it seeks to change its world. In terms of gender, it is hardly surprising that there are some who simply do not fit neatly into the categorical system that allows *das Man* to operate smoothly. For such cases, gender breaks down, and innovation is needed if their lives are to be rendered intelligible. Such individuals are, as a result of their specific orientation in the world, excluded from *das Man* and are impelled to resolutely challenge norms and take an authentic stance with regard to their gender, as well as on gender issues in general, as a public issue, and the larger community of *das Man* that values the gender norms that exclude them. Their challenges, if successful, will soon enough be incorporated into the common sense of *das Man*, and they can eventually gain social acceptance by means of transgression and visibility. An example of this might be found in the gay rights movement in the United States. In 1969, there was a raid on the Stonewall Inn, a bar on Christopher Street in New York City. The police raided the bar because some of its patrons violated the current laws against cross-dressing. This sparked a riot in the short term, but in the long term, it generated a political and social movement seeking legal acceptance of homosexuals. Today, homosexuals are increasingly (although by no means universally) accepted in the United States, and *das Man* increasingly frowns on discriminating against homosexuals.[46] Laws against cross-dressing and sodomy have been struck down by the courts, and sex reassignment surgery has become, if not exactly common, at least a practical possibility for those who need it and can afford it. The cost of these developments has been the repudiation of cross-dressers and transsexual persons by factions of both the gay rights and the women's rights movements. Those who transgress gender norms in ways other than homosexuality have to fight many of the same battles over again to gain recognition of our own possibilities of Being.

When Dasein finds itself in the position of transgressor, it may well be abjected and disregarded (indeed, discarded) by *das Man*, or it may discover that the persistence of other transgressors creates the possibility of their becoming heroes to future individuals, which has the potential to alter the face of the social, ethical, and political context by disclosing options that have not been previously apparent. The very existence of non-gender-conforming individuals has the potential to disclose that the sex and gender binaries presupposed by *das Man* are not, in fact, universal truths and that other possibilities for Being-in-the-world are available.

Gender and Freedom

In being gendered, then, individuals find themselves situated in a particular way in the world, engaged in a futurally oriented in-order-to structure of possibilities, within a culture that provides readymade norms and expectations placed on each individual. The phenomenological conception of freedom is the context within which choice is rendered possible and intelligible, the field of possibility within which Dasein operates.[47] Freedom lies less in the particular choices Dasein makes than in the possibility for making choice at all. How transgressive (or conforming) Dasein chooses to play out its life within the field of its own possibilities is where its freedom lies, not in whether it will be so oriented in this field. This point is richly illustrated by McWhorter:

> Coming out was not a liberating experience for me—or rather, it was only liberating in some ways and for some parts of me; in the main, I experienced it as an acknowledgment of defeat and as a surrender to a socially constructed identity that brought with it a set of strict limitations, expectations, and requirements over which I had little control. I chose it because I finally admitted that I had no choice. My resistance had been futile in the face of such vast networks of social power. I had failed.[48]

McWhorter's orientation is such that she was unable to remain "in the closet" without serious consequences to her well-being. But the act of coming out of the closet, of acknowledging herself as transgressive, is something she resisted because the individual free choice of coming out involves much more than mere acknowledgment and affirmation of desire or sexual orientation. It involves allowing oneself to be defined by *das Man* as a transgressor and taking responsibility for this. It also involves accepting the entire discourse in which sexual desire is a significant facet of identity, whether one agrees with this characterization of human identity or not, since this is an integral part of the field of possibility and freedom. Seating one's identity—even partly—in sexuality is a characterization perpetuated by the dominant discourse of *das Man*, which makes up the horizon of possibility or freedom. This can be constraining at times, particularly for the transgender or transsexual individual who does not understand himself according to the all-too-Cartesian "stuck in the wrong body" trope. Why can one not be an embodied transsexual person who acknowledges his past instead? Well, one can—but at the expense of making sense to most people.

What Dasein has to work with, then, is its own thrown situatedness, its own orientation, and the world, which is composed of things and others. While each individual is uniquely situated in the world, the world itself is a point of commonality and horizon of possibility for all members of any community. Insofar as physical perceptions are concerned, norms act as the point of reference, and individuals are rendered intelligible according to how closely or distantly they conform to norms, which are abstractions and function as the most reliable version of a given thing, as well as according to their situatedness in perception and relation to the body.

Cultural norms are not so very different from perceptual norms in that they are also means of organizing perceptions and behaviors, of classifying phenomena, and thus of rendering them intelligible. Phenomena that are disclosed as part of a world, or a context of meaningfulness, in which they make sense are understood. When Dasein encounters a behavior in itself or others, it interprets this behavior in a way that makes sense with regard to cultural norms. So when Dasein encounters another Dasein who behaves in a way that is culturally understood to be masculine, the tendency is to ascribe both masculinity and maleness to the individual, unless other factors are present that confuse or obscure the issue. When the issue is not clear-cut, the individual in question is rendered unintelligible, an oddity who is all too commonly abjected, pathologized, or mocked. If, however, enough cases of transgression appear, then they challenge the norm and are themselves rendered intelligible by means of the expansion of norms to include the phenomena encountered. As Merleau-Ponty points out, human being is Being-sexual, and existence and sexuality are so interpermeated as to render the phenomena inseparable.[49] Sexuality is both a cause and an effect of Dasein's deportment in the world, and I argue that the same can be said of gender. In fact, gender is the more public of the two phenomena, and it is, therefore, the point at which Dasein's immediate correspondence to others is most apparent. The more visible aspects of biological sex can, with more or less ease, be hidden or changed, but it is very difficult indeed to conceal gender, precisely because gender is played out in interactions with others. (This is why sex reassignment surgery is an available option—nobody has found a way to change anybody's gender at will, but ways to change bodies are available. Sex reassignment surgeries help bring the physical body into line or accordance with personal or social expectations regarding the relationship of sex and gender.) Just as sexual identity is accounted for not by mere biology but also by the social context, the *Mitsein* in which Dasein always already finds itself, gender is not only a characteristic of individuals but also the way that bodies indicate and perpetuate relationships within *das Man*. Dasein, as embodied Being, is the site in which gendered appearance and meaningfulness are established and occur.

The relationship between perceptual norms and cultural norms is a tightly interwoven one. The way Dasein perceives phenomena is largely influenced by the conceptual, even political, models that render phenomena intelligible to it. At the same time, the conceptual-political model thrives only as long as it successfully describes reality, or *a* reality. As long as a paradigm or model allows Dasein to understand its experience of the world, it thrives. When a model is challenged by the obtrusion of exceptions into visibility, the model itself no longer facilitates Dasein's understanding of actual experience. It breaks down and becomes conspicuous *as* a model, which is then examined, dissected, and questioned. When this occurs, Dasein's perceptions, as well as cultural mores, can be affected. For example, when the dominant model of the universe held that Earth was at the center, astronomers *saw* and attempted to give an account of heavenly bodies changing direction. When the dominant model changed, and it was understood that Earth revolves around the sun, then what astronomers *saw* was different orbits from different perspectives causing heavenly bodies to move in more easily predictable patterns. This made a difference for Dasein in many spheres of its experience, and not merely for those Dasein who were physicists, as Galileo was well aware. The sense data in both cases are the same, but the perceptions are understood differently.

In the case of sex and gender, too, when the continuing discourse about a model undergoes changes, it also discloses the possibility of changing Dasein's understanding and, in a very real way, changing Dasein itself in significant ways. As Foucault points out in *The History of Sexuality*, discourses surrounding sexuality have blossomed, proliferating concepts and vocabularies, and have become firmly established as foundational to identity. Discourses surrounding gender do the same, which is hardly surprising given that they predate the discourses that Foucault describes. And because there has been a proliferation of concepts that account for Dasein's possibilities for being since the Enlightenment, there is also a proliferation of ways in which Dasein can potentially transgress the norms established by the discourse. "The limit and transgression depend on each other for whatever density of being they possess: a limit could not exist if it were absolutely uncrossable and, reciprocally, transgression would be pointless if it merely crossed a limit composed of illusions and shadows."[50] The change Dasein undergoes when it understands itself according to a different conceptual model is a real change, and the possibility of transgression is necessary to the establishment of a norm.

Dasein finds itself always already thrown into the world and horizon of possibilities that shape it, possessing the capacity to choose what to do with the way it finds itself so oriented, and therein lies both a greater and a lesser freedom than is generally supposed. The freedom is lesser because it is rarely a matter of choice between options that Dasein might prefer; it is certainly never a radically free choice, since it must be made within an existing world, a community, and a discourse if it is to be intelligible. An individual Dasein who finds itself so oriented as to be transgressive might have the freedom to choose to remain closeted or to declare its transgression to the world, but it does not have the choice to *be* transgressive or *not be* transgressive.

The freedom is also greater because individuals do have the discourse at their disposal, too, and each Dasein has its effect on the discourse, the operations of power, and the very conceptual frameworks employed by *das Man*. Transgression is disclosive of the way power operates, and thus transgressive Dasein, simply by being transgressive, has the potential to disclose and deploy operations of power in ways that create new possibilities for deployment. Individuals constitute discourses of power, and the existence and visibility of transgressors have the capacity to affect the ways in which power is deployed. As transgressions are identified, the models employed by the dominant discourse either accommodate them or pathologize them, but they cannot ignore them. Noninclusion happens only with phenomena that do not matter. This means that Dasein is not doomed to cultural determinism but, rather, is an active participant in the construction of the conceptual models according to which it understands itself and the world. This is nothing less than freedom, since freedom is not mere choice, but the very condition of the possibility of choice, within a meaningful world, shaped by history, and with an eye toward the future.

The story of gender, then, of what femininity and masculinity are and how they are meaningful to Dasein's Being, is a story played out at a very

fundamental level in Dasein's ontology. The tension between the individuation of factical Being and its participation in *das Man* arises out of the clash
between Dasein's tendencies toward both heterogeneity and homogeneity.
Butler's account of gender as a social construction resonates with Heidegger's
description of how *das Man* enframes Dasein, providing the conceptual structure for how Dasein thinks of itself. In repetition, gender norms become en-
trenched in the expectations of *das Man* and in Dasein's understanding of
itself and its place in the world. These expectations become both the means of
achieving disciplined conformity to *das Man* and the loci of resistance to such
conformity, which appears as various types of transgression and innovation.
When norms are expanded through transgression, this does nothing less than
make it possible for Dasein to Be in more ways—freedom increases. The proliferation of criteria for sex assignment has effected a proliferation of intersex
conditions. No less does the proliferation of intelligible gender transgressions
effect a proliferation of potential ways of Being-in-the-world.

NOTES

1. And, of course, essentialism holds that there is something essential to masculinity, maleness, and men, as well.
2. See Luce Irigaray, "This Sex Which Is Not One," in *This Sex Which Is Not One*, trans. Catherine Porter and Carolyn Burke (Ithaca, NY: Cornell University Press, 1985), 27; and Nel Noddings, *Caring: A Feminine Approach to Ethics and Moral Education* (Berkeley: University of California Press, 1984).
3. Gayatri Chakravorty Spivak, "In a Word: Interview," interview by Ellen Rooney, in *The Essential Difference*, ed. Naomi Schor and Elizabeth Weed (Bloomington: Indiana University Press, 1994), 152.
4. See Irigaray, *This Sex Which Is Not One*, 23–33.
5. Heidegger, *Being and Time*, 86; H. 59.
6. See Judith Butler, "Dangerous Crossings: Willa Cather's Masculine Names," in *Bodies That Matter* (New York: Routledge, 1993), 143–166.
7. Many transgender and transsexual people find this popular characterization to be inadequate for describing their experience of gender. Some use much stronger language than "inadequate."
8. Martin Heidegger, "Memorial Address," in *Discourse on Thinking*, trans. John M. Anderson and E. Hans Freund (New York: Harper and Row, 1966), 50. See also Janssen, "Queering Heidegger."
9. Martin Heidegger, "Only a God Can Save Us: *Der Spiegel*'s Interview with Martin Heidegger," *Philosophy Today* 20, no. 4 (1976): 276.
10. Martin Heidegger, "The Turning," in *The Question Concerning Technology*, trans. William Lovitt (New York: Harper and Row, 1977), 48.
11. Martin Heidegger, "The Question Concerning Technology," in *Basic Writings*, ed. David Farrell Krell, trans. William Lovitt (San Francisco: HarperCollins, 1993), 339.

12. Heidegger, "Memorial Address," 53.

13. See Heidegger, "The Question Concerning Technology"; and Heidegger, "Memorial Address."

14. Ladelle McWhorter, *Bodies and Pleasures: Foucault and the Politics of Sexual Normalization* (Indianapolis: Indiana University Press, 1999), 156.

15. Simone de Beauvoir, *The Ethics of Ambiguity*, trans. Bernard Frechtman (New York: Citadel Press, 1948), 17–18.

16. Ibid., 49–50 (emphasis in original).

17. Catherine Saillant, "School Blamed in Killing of Gay Student," *Los Angeles Times*, May 8, 2008, http://www.latimes.com/news/printedition/california/la-me-oxnard8 -2008may08,0,6901056.story.

18. Ashley Fantz, "An Ohio Transgender Teen's Suicide, a Mother's Anguish," *CNN*, January 4, 2015, http://www.cnn.com/2014/12/31/us/ohio-transgender-teen-suicide/.

19. Judith Butler, "Phantasmatic Identification and the Assumption of Sex," in *Bodies That Matter* (New York: Routledge, 1993), 115.

20. Butler, *Gender Trouble*, 23.

21. Heidegger, *Being and Time*, 360; H. 312.

22. Butler, *Gender Trouble*, 43–44.

23. Judith Butler, "Introduction," in *Bodies That Matter* (New York: Routledge, 1993), 2.

24. Judith Butler, "Arguing with the Real," in *Bodies That Matter* (New York: Routledge, 1993), 187.

25. The "abject" "designates here precisely those 'unlivable' and 'uninhabitable' zones of social life which are nevertheless densely populated by those who do not enjoy the status of the subject, but whose living under the sign of the 'unlivable' is required to circumscribe the domain of the subject." Judith Butler, "Introduction," 3.

26. Judith Butler, "Phantasmatic Identification," 94.

27. Ibid., 107.

28. Ibid.

29. For examples and analyses of this phenomenon, see Janice Raymond, *The Transsexual Empire: The Making of the She-Male* (New York: Teachers College Press, 1994); Judith Halberstam, "Transgender Butch: Butch/FTM Border Wars and the Masculine Continuum," *GLQ: A Journal of Lesbian and Gay Studies* 4, no. 2 (1998): 287–310; Stephen Whittle, "Where Did We Go Wrong? Feminism and Trans Theory—Two Teams on the Same Side," in *The Transgender Studies Reader*, ed. Susan Stryker and Stephen Whittle (New York: Routledge, 2006), 194–204; Paul Vitello, "The Trouble When Jane Becomes Jack," *New York Times*, August 20, 2006, http://query.nytimes.com/gst/fullpage.html? res=9802EEDD153EF933A1575BC0A9609C8B63; and Susan Stryker, *Transgender History* (Berkeley, CA: Seal Studies, 2008), 91–120.

30. "Only in terms of an orientation towards the ontological structure thus conceived can 'life' as a state of Being be defined *a priori*, and this must be done in a privative manner. Ontically as well as ontologically, the priority belongs to Being-in-the-world as concern." Heidegger, *Being and Time*, 85; H. 58.

31. "I want to ask how and why 'materiality' has become a sign of irreducibility, that is, how is it that the materiality of sex is understood as that which only bears cultural constructions and, therefore, cannot be a construction?" Judith Butler, "Bodies That Matter," in *Bodies That Matter* (New York: Routledge, 1993), 28.

32. Heidegger, *Being and Time*, 438; H. 386.

33. Butler, *Gender Trouble*, 179 (emphasis in original).

34. See Sarah Blaffer Hrdy, *Mother Nature: A History of Mothers, Infants, and Natural Selection* (New York: Vintage, 2000).

35. Butler, *Gender Trouble*, 42.

36. Ibid., 41.

37. "Indeed, part of the pleasure, the giddiness of the performance is in the recognition of a radical contingency in the relation between sex and gender in the face of cultural configurations of causal unities that are regularly assumed to be natural and necessary." Ibid., 175.

38. Ibid., 181.

39. Heidegger, *Being and Time*, 272; H. 229 (emphasis in original).

40. Butler, *Gender Trouble*, 189.

41. Butler, "Preface," x.

42. Heidegger, *Being and Time*, 329; H. 283.

43. Ibid., 232; H. 187.

44. "Only by historicality which is factical and authentic can the history of what has-been-there, as a resolute fate, be disclosed in such a manner that in repetition the 'force' of the possible gets struck home into one's factical existence—in other words, that it comes towards that existence in its futural character." Ibid., 447; H. 395.

45. Ibid., 173; H. 134.

46. There is still a lot of work to be done, but the changes in the general public attitude toward gay people in the past decade or so are striking.

47. "What is freedom? To be born is to be born of the world and to be born into the world. The world is already constituted, but also never completely constituted; in the first case we are acted upon, in the second we are open to an infinite number of possibilities. But this analysis is still abstract, for we exist in both ways *at once*." Merleau-Ponty, *Phenomenology of Perception*, 527 (emphasis in original).

48. McWhorter, *Bodies and Pleasures*, 106.

49. Merleau-Ponty, *Phenomenology of Perception*, 196.

50. Michel Foucault, "A Preface to Transgression," 73.

CHAPTER 5

GENDER, TECHNOLOGY, AND STYLE

WHEW! THE QUESTION of gender is clearly not as simple as it looks on the surface. One last question that demands attention here is whether gender is a primordial ontological structure of Dasein or merely an ontical contingency that happens to obtain in Dasein. In other words, is gender intrinsic to Dasein's being Dasein? Or is gender to be found entirely in the detail and surface of Dasein's life? This is another version of the nature-nurture question, which is generally how questions regarding gender are framed. It is also another binary. I reject the dualistic construction of the question, which is usually asked as though the phenomenon of gender must be one type of phenomenon to the exclusion of the other. Instead, I submit the following accounting of gender: *Gender is a style of Being, shaped by the tensions that obtain between individuating Dasein, understandings of embodiment, and the social constructs according to which Dasein's Being is rendered intelligible, and operating according to deployments of power by means of technologies.* Gender permeates both the ontical and the ontological and has implications for both Dasein's innate, primordial structure and its ontical concerns. The observable aspects of gender, who wears skirts and who wears kilts, for instance, are ontical. They have to do with the details of Dasein's involvement *as* entities and *with* entities, in a specific historical situation, and performed by individuated, embodied, and uniquely oriented Dasein. But the implications of transgressing and questioning gender reverberate to Dasein's ontological character; these questions shake Dasein to its very Being by challenging some of the most basic presuppositions Dasein has about Being itself and questioning the contextual structures of gender within which such things as skirts and kilts exist.

While it is not fundamental to Dasein's ontology that it divide all individuals into men and women, it *is* fundamental to Dasein's ontology that *das Man* divide, distinguish, and differentiate between individuals, that categories of one sort or another be established, maintained, and challenged by transgression. It is not fundamental to Dasein's ontology that heteronormativity reign supreme, but it *is* fundamental to Dasein's ontology to be engaged in some processes of normativity and transgression because transgression and alternative possibility are the ways in which technologies and power are deployed in Dasein's engagement with the world. Without transgression, norms cannot arise, and without norms, Being is not rendered intelligible. It is not fundamental to Dasein's ontology that any of the classifications that currently exist be the classifications that are used, but it is fundamental that Dasein establish classifications at all, whether based in similarity, difference, resemblance, or exclusion, in order to facilitate the questioning that reveals truths. Is Dasein gendered? It certainly is. Is it necessary that Dasein always and for all time be gendered according to current biological, social, or legal constructs? Not in the least. The classifications that will occur in the future are unpredictable in our current historical situation, but they will no doubt occur in their own time.

Dasein's Got Style!

There is this phenomenon, by which members of a community are typed and rendered intelligible in relation to others, in which power is deployed and resisted, varied, deployed, and resisted again. Gender is one of the ways in which existence is given shape and becomes meaningful Being. This shape is built on a framework (*Gestell*) of thinking, part of the background of the lived world, which Heidegger characterizes as "technology" and which both "brings forth truth into the splendor of radiant appearance"[1] and, when Dasein limits itself to technological thinking, "threatens revealing, threatens it with the possibility that all revealing will present itself only in the unconcealment of standing-reserve."[2] Gender arises out of the tension that obtains between the they-self and its individuated orientation in-the-world. In other words, gender is a social phenomenon that takes place at the site of intersection between individuals and their cultural contexts.

Foucault seizes on Heidegger's description of the operations of technology and refines it further, describing the various kinds of technologies that contribute to Dasein's understanding of itself and the world:

> (1) technologies of production, which permit us to produce, transform, or manipulate things; (2) technologies of sign systems, which permit us to use signs, meanings, symbols, or signification; (3) technologies of power, which determine the conduct of individuals and submit them to certain ends or domination, an objectivizing of the subject; (4) technologies of the self, which permit individuals to effect by their own means, or with the help of others, a certain number of operations on their own bodies and souls, thoughts, conduct, and way of being, so as to transform themselves in order to attain a certain state of happiness, purity, wisdom, perfection, or immortality.[3]

These technologies do not operate discretely; they are interconnected and interreliant, to be found in varying degrees in the sundry phenomena of Dasein's Being. The first two types of technology have to do with the sciences and linguistics.[4] Technologies of power are those technologies by means of which authority or lack thereof are established. Legal status and social role are examples of these. Medicine, self-discipline, and ethical systems are the means by which individuals take care of themselves, cultivating well-being of body and soul. Foucault characterizes these means as "technologies of the self."[5] All the ways in which Dasein understands and disciplines itself, and all the ways in which the tendencies toward *Gestell* and transgression produce relationships, power, individuality, norms, trends, and transgression are driven by technologies that govern entities. Language (broadly construed), relationships among cases of Dasein, and the various genera of power provide the means for endless variation on the stylistic themes Dasein produces with them.

Applying the ontological concepts of style and technology to how a transsexual individual can understand himself may elucidate how these technologies relate to one another. Rather than speak for another, I will use myself as an example, with the caveat that this is one factical instance and not representative of all trans experience: I am, just like everyone else, uniquely oriented in the world, and my orientation is more radically atypical than most in that my understanding of my own gender differs from that which is expected by my culture. I was assigned biologically female at birth but understand myself to be a man. The technologies I employ in my transition to the masculine gender can be understood according to the genera of technologies as Foucault has laid them out: (1) the transformation and manipulation of body (as a thing) through exercise, diet, hormones, and surgery to produce maleness; (2) employment of signs to indicate social role, particularly changing legal identification and clothing; (3) employment of technologies of power in conduct, including the assumption of the role of "man" within society and changing both name and legal status; and (4) transformation of self by means of these technologies into a Dasein who is recognizably a man, in my own and my communities' understandings of what that means. These technologies may overlap, as with the assumption of the legal status of "man," which is a manipulation of both technologies of power and also of technologies of signs. Within the field of options available, identification as a woman was intolerable, so I have taken a different direction and am living in a style that is understood as being "manhood." This is not to say there is no opposition to my transgender status but only that such a transition as the one I have undergone is culturally intelligible *as* a transition into the complex phenomenon called "manhood." The gender transition itself is somewhat transgressive in that it is undertaken at all. But the *terms* of the transition are the cultural markers that I adopted in this transgressive transition by means of technologies within the field of possibility that defines them as "masculine." There are those who refuse to accept me as a man and who insist on my being a "woman." Even to these people, however, I am a force to be reckoned with in ways that women typically are not. Opposition only underscores how deeply invested in traditional gender roles the general public is. To date, I have faced nothing worse than threats, scorn, workplace discrimination, and familial disapprobation. Others are not so fortunate. Trans women of color, in particular, often experience the intersection of race, class, and gender as a site of precarious and violent vulnerability. This deplorable state of affairs is an indication that gender transition causes a great deal of upset for some factions of society. Violent reaction is also a symptom of a society being forced to confront a state of affairs that it has taken for granted as necessary but that is proving to be contingent. Threats may indicate resistance to an inevitable reconceptualization of gender that is already well under way in Western culture in the twenty-first century. This resistance is an acknowledgement of the danger inherent in the challenge of *Gestell*, but it is in this danger, as Heidegger shows us, that the saving power of revealed truth also lies.

What trans individuals are doing, in phenomenological terms, is reiterating and citing norms that establish intelligibility while also innovating on these same norms in such a way as to challenge the very definitions of normality provided by *das Man*. The possibility of transgression is always at the heart of the demand for conformity to norms, and this gives rise to a tension that does much more than merely command legitimation of the feminine in a world that privileges the masculine. Tradition demands that transgression exist and be visible, while at the same time punishing its existence and visibility. Transgressive Dasein, in Being-not-normal, does not contradict or obliterate the norm. Rather, the transgressor pushes against the boundaries of definition, varying the themes that are provided by *das Man* and creating the conditions in which intelligibility and meaningfulness may arise by challenging the hegemony of the norm. This results in uncanniness for all those involved, forcing an authentic evaluation of the kind of transgression the transgressor represents. The possibility of a man born female alters the field of possibility for everyone: the equation of maleness with masculinity encounters resistance, and this resistance becomes a new site of the interplay of power that defines gender for all.

The themes and variations on themes played out in the deployment of technology are what several thinkers (Merleau-Ponty, Foucault, Husserl, and Butler) refer to as "style." There are, of course, important differences in their theories of style, but there are also significant similarities, which allow me to use it here primarily as a theoretical concept that is related to the phenomenological understanding of freedom. In its phenomenological sense, the term "style" refers to more than mere fashions in clothing, music, and the like, although it is certainly manifested in such phenomena. Style is, rather, the direction taken in the field of possibility that is freedom; it is the shape that all these employments of technologies and operations of power take. They must, after all, take *some* form or other. Within this field of possibility, Dasein chooses—or is already oriented toward, or is predisposed to more readily understand—some options, and others are left behind. And since the way Dasein does this is by variation on themes, that which is varied and the variations themselves take on a shape, a style.

Merleau-Ponty describes style, in "Indirect Language and the Voices of Silence," as being

> the primary operation which first constitutes signs as signs, makes that which is expressed dwell in them through the eloquence of their arrangement and configuration alone, implants a meaning in that which did not have one, and thus—far from exhausting itself in the instant at which it occurs—inaugurates an order and founds an institution or tradition.[6]

This is not only applicable to works of art, however. It is also applicable to relational phenomena such as gender. Phenomena are intelligible within a context of what is already established, whether as an institution, a tradition, or a norm; Dasein understands differences and variations, as well as repetitions, as being part of what has gone before, as being meaningfully related to what is already well understood, or at least widely accepted. Style is the prerequisite for signs to be constituted, a necessary condition for any kind of meaningfulness to be produced by Dasein in its facticity. Dasein always already finds itself living according to some style or other, whether it is plunking along comfortably in its fallen state or facing up to its anxiety and discomfort in authentic resoluteness.

Husserl addresses the issue of style as it applies to the individual, in terms of the "style of a life," pointing out that there is something more or less permanent or characteristic of each individual, without resorting to substance, that allows one "to a certain extent [to] expect how a man will behave in a given case if one has correctly apperceived him in his person, in his style."[7] That is, style is not only something that provides life with a general shape and direction but also something that is available to Dasein to use in understanding and more or less reliably predicting events in the world and the behavior of others. An individual's style, or character, functions something akin to perceptual norm for Husserl; it is that according to which particulars—in this case, particular behaviors—are rendered intelligible and predictable. If one knows, for instance, that Mr. Jones avoids spiders whenever possible and breaks out in a cold sweat when they are impossible to avoid, then one can reasonably expect him to decline an invitation to spend a pleasant evening viewing a documentary about arachnids. When there are anomalies in an individual's behavior, those actions are rendered intelligible *as* discrepancies from the individual's usual style. If Mr. Jones does choose to view several documentaries about arachnids, one might reasonably assume that he is trying to cure himself of his arachnophobia. Inductive logic relies heavily on an understanding of style to craft expectations in and of the lived world.

When Butler describes gender as "the repeated stylization of the body, a set of repeated acts within a highly rigid regulatory frame that congeal over time to produce the appearance of substance, of a natural sort of being,"[8] she is not saying that gender is mere mimicry or parody (although parody can be one form of gender performance). She is applying the phenomenological notion of style to the issue of gender. Gender is stylized performance of behavior, performed by bodies, which renders individuals' behavior intelligible within a context that itself constitutes a field of possibilities. This field of intelligible possibilities establishes norms constituted by the repetition of certain kinds of acts, while the repetition of these kinds of acts also generates expectations of future repetition. The net result of style is a social construction that is constitutive of individual Dasein's way of Being and also constituted by Dasein.

All this is not to say that style is immutable; far from it. What makes the idea of style so helpful to the question of gender is that it does not rely on clearly delineated definitions of phenomena but, rather, is concerned with the relationships of resemblance and divergence *among* phenomena. Style begets what Wittgenstein describes as "family resemblances"[9] between things, rather than discrete concepts. And since the phenomenologist examines gender as it occurs in lived experience, this is exactly the form gender can be expected to take. Gender arises out of relationships that obtain within the social order, as governed by ever-shifting and ever-correcting technologies of power, which render experience intelligible. In short, gender is one style of Dasein's Being-in-the-world-with-others. The details of any given style of gender are neither universal nor absolute. Conceptions of gender do change according to the needs of society and the context in which gender is understood, but it is the case that Dasein's Being always takes some shape or other in relation to others and in relation to the world, so Dasein's Being is always shaped according to some style, to some gender, by which Dasein can distinguish between individuals and understand its own particular, factical orientation in-the-world. Reiteration of themes does establish the *Gestell*, or framework, that renders its own Being intelligible to it. But Dasein, being futurally oriented, does not merely repeat the past when it is engaged in stylistic repetition. The past does provide the possibility of repetition in Dasein's present, in a different factical situation and orientation, which is to say, in a way that bears stylistic resemblance to its past but varies the past to accommodate the needs of the present and plans for the future.

This operation is not a utopia-aimed historical progression but a knotted web of interactions between various and sometimes surprisingly related technologies. When looking at the ways gender was constructed in past ages, it is necessary to simultaneously keep in mind both the alterity of the past and the continuity between the past and present in history. On one hand, there is a great deal to be learned from the kinds of shifts that have occurred in the way gender has been conceived, but on the other, the current age is heir to these conceptions, and they do form each subsequent age's cultural heritage. When one analyzes the genders that existed in Ancient Greece, for instance, it helps a great deal to note that Greek ethical systems were more preoccupied with excess and temperance than with the condemnation or approbation of specific acts, and to understand that they involved not just than men and women but also boys and *kinaidoi*.[10] The *kinaidos* was less than fully masculine, not because he was the recipient of penetrative sex acts but because he was assumed to overindulge in pleasure. To be masculine in terms of both gender and sex among the Greeks involved self-rule and self-control in a way that is not exactly paralleled by the currently dominant Abrahamic conception of ethics, which so often places moral value on particular acts. One danger of this sort of phenomenological investigation is, of course, that of reading history through the historian's own conceptions of human experience, politics, history, and other conceptual frameworks, thus obscuring the most informative differences between Dasein of the past and of the present. Another danger lies in identifying existing practices as "obsolete" or simple remnants of history, thus marginalizing them and denying their legitimacy in informing later styles of Being. At the same time, there is a great deal to be learned from examining historical constructions *as* social constructions, rather than as way stations on the road of progress or nostalgically longed-for golden ages. Each age has its dominant discourses, its own set of technologies that interact and inform one another. These are nothing more or less than the aspects of life that matter most to those living in that age, both because the technologies engender the discourses by which life is intelligible and because they matter to those whose age they shape. Technologies shape the style of Dasein's Being; they alter and shift because Dasein becomes concerned with aspects of life that are not satisfactorily accounted for by the ordinary conception of things, by *das Man*. And so Dasein's orientation and work are turned in the direction of its needs and desires, but there are always new needs and new desires to address, and thus new technologies will always arise and Dasein's style will always be in flux. Dasein's historical situation is both the exploration of Being and the production of meaningfulness, which generates new aspects of being to explore. As Merleau-Ponty puts it:

> Human life is not played upon a single scale. There are echoes and exchanges between one scale and another; but a given man who has never confronted passions faces up to history, another who thinks in an ordinary way is free with *mores*, and another one who lives to all appearances like everybody else has thoughts which uproot all things.[11]

All individuals, whether their lives play radical variations on the themes or not, also play on the scales made available by the givenness of nature, culture, language, and norms. The way these themes and styles are played out lies in the technologies Dasein employs, the discourses Dasein deploys, and the individuated lives that all lead within the ontological field of possibility that is Dasein's freedom.

Technology: The Dangerous and the Bad

If style is understood as being the direction Dasein's freedom takes, technology can be understood as the means of implementing this freedom in a particular direction.[12] On my reading, Heidegger's account of technology supports the thesis that style is central to any examination of Dasein's Being. In "The Question Concerning Technology," he lays out the problem of technology as such and of technological thinking. When he does this, he uses the language of traditional metaphysics, which is curious given that Heidegger's lifelong philosophical project is to challenge and deconstruct traditional metaphysics and all the problems to which it gives rise. Why does he do this, if not to demonstrate that traditional metaphysical thinking is itself subject to the danger he warns against in the essay—limiting thinking by convincing us all that there is no other legitimate way to think? He asks why Aristotle mentions only four types of cause, and he points out that "so long as we do not allow ourselves to go into these questions, causality, and with it instrumentality, and with this the accepted definition of technology, remain obscure and groundless."[13] Traditional metaphysics is one example of a *Gestell* on which Dasein constructs its philosophical endeavors and the meaningfulness of factical life. Calculative thinking, the kind of thinking that measures and quantifies, is another example. When Dasein takes certain ways of thinking for granted, it does not see the possibilities for other ways of thinking. When this happens, Dasein does not know that which it does not know and is rendered bereft of the possibility for making inquiries in a different direction, and its inquiries are guided in a direction that excludes the possibility of other kinds of seeking.[14]

This is precisely what Heidegger warns of in the essay: not gadgetry, not traditional metaphysics, but the limiting of Dasein's capacity for thinking in certain ways. He uses technology as an example but also cleverly asks the question in such a way that traditional metaphysics is employed to exemplify the danger. And what form does the warning take? For all his use of language that characterizes technological thinking as a danger, Heidegger never says that technological thinking is bad or undesirable. Technology and even technological thinking have the capacity to build new conceptual frameworks at least as much as they have the power to limit thought. The dangerous, it would seem, is not the same as the bad. And technological thinking *is* dangerous, when a given discourse is taken to be the sole, or the primary, legitimate approach. Furthermore, technology alters Dasein's Being; it has the capacity to alter the very means by which Dasein is engaged with its world and with others. The ontological nearness of others in spite of physical estrangement, the availability of information, and the possibility for traveling the world are all examples of how specific technological advances, as well as technological thinking, have altered Dasein's way of Being-in-the-world-with-others.[15] This capacity to alter is where the real danger lies, because it means Dasein is not in control of technology any more than it is in control of any other dominant discourse. Technology in its essence is no mere tool to be employed as Dasein wishes, whether to feed the hungry or to more efficiently commit genocide. Rather, it is the means of enacting and living the styles of Being in which Dasein is actively engaged, and as such, it directs not only Dasein's inquiries but also the presuppositions on which its inquiries are founded and the types of answers that may be sought. Technology is outside Dasein's control in a very real way precisely because it shapes Dasein's capacity for inquiry; it does not tell Dasein what to think but rather tells Dasein how to think and what things are worth thinking about. In doing so, technology shapes and styles the revealing power (*aletheia*) of human thought, which is nothing less than the establishment of truth itself.

For all the danger presented by technology and technological thinking, there is also a promised "saving power" to be found within it.[16] *Gestell* directs Dasein's thinking in a certain direction, according to a certain style, and at the same time, since truths are disclosed and established by the direction of inquiry, the capacity for thinking further is also ensured. Dasein's Being must take some style or other, after all, and the capacity of technology to alter this style of Being is a capacity that any other discourse shares. Here is where the saving power lies: there are always multiple discourses at work in Dasein's Being, also disclosing the world and establishing truth. In "The Question Concerning Technology," Heidegger isolates one discourse to elucidate the power that any discourse has over shaping the style of Dasein's Being, but in actual fact, Being is never isolated to only one aspect. Being is always already made up of interreliant and interconnecting ways of thinking, and all these ways of thinking stand to affect and be affected by technology, particularly as the ones engaged in this multifaceted thinking are themselves uniquely oriented in the world and bring their own individuated perspectives to what is and can be thought. To be sure, this is dangerous. We are as wanton in our explorations as children at play in a laboratory, and there is no adult in charge to keep an eye out for our safety. But the danger is the necessary condition for the revealing of truth, and the saving power lies in recognizing the styles and discourses generated by metaphysics, by technological thinking, and by all other aspects of Being as discourses that generate more questions, rather than accepting them as immutable truth. Once Dasein believes it has found absolute truth, it stops looking for what can be revealed and occupies itself with mere ordering of what is known. But questioning must always be questioning *about* something, so some stability is necessary for Dasein to engage in thinking. There is another point of tension here, between Dasein's tendency toward the stability of *Gestell* on one hand and the drive to question and reveal on the other. Toward the end of his essay on technology, Heidegger compares this tension to "the paths of two stars in the course of the heavens. But precisely this, their passing by, is the hidden side of their nearness."[17] Both are needed for the revealing of truth to occur; indeed, each is necessary for the other to exist and maintain its path through the heavens. Together, they are what shape the course that Dasein's thinking takes, and it is the way Dasein thinks that is precisely what establishes its style of Being.

The *Gestell* of gender, deployed as many technologies, is what establishes Dasein's Being in such a way that it is understood according to certain parameters—as related to embodiment, as one of the many individuating principles that distinguishes *this* Dasein from *that* one, as a contingent set of mutually exclusive possibilities, as mutable according to social needs and the courses taken by dominant discourses, and as the tension that arises between the already established and the disclosive. This is where transgressive Dasein comes in and illuminates the discourses already at work and taken for granted in the operations of power that shape and give style to Being; those who transgress the expectations of *das Man* as a result of their particular and unique individuated orientations in the world are engaged, willingly or not, in revealing the contingency of the way living beings are ordered into the categories of male-female, masculine-feminine. Transgressors create tension with already established truths by revealing the way they shape Dasein's thinking from the start. And what happens when gender-transgressive Dasein is taken into account, when the *Gestell* that shapes thinking is reframed, except that more questions arise? This is an indication that this line of questioning is onto something important, as questioning the gender binary leads to questions of how the transgression of that binary will be dealt with by the legal system, by schools, by medical communities. It leads to issues of marketing, since the presupposition that there are men and there are women and they purchase different products comes under scrutiny. It leads to issues of construction and building, as the demand for bathrooms to accommodate those who fit into neither traditional gender role grows. It leads to issues of child rearing, since parents have had occasion to question whether their children are, in fact, boys or girls, not to mention how much it matters to them that their children be unambiguously one or the other. It leads to issues of human identity and just how fundamentally linked to gender it is. And, what I find most interesting of all, this robust, lived resistance of the gender binary leads to questions about how the most foundational understanding of self and world has come to take the style it has and also about how both might be understood differently. The questions raised by gender transgression go on and on. But then, questioning is itself the sign that there are issues to be resolved. Nobody questions that which is already fully understood; nor do people question that which is unimportant. Questions arise about those aspects of Being that have yet to be revealed, with which Dasein is already meaningfully involved, which cause trouble because they involve contradiction or oppress individuals. It is in questioning that the potentiality for truths to be revealed is fostered. Here, a third level of transgression is most significant: that of deliberately making my own story public. The more of us who do this, the more of us force *das Man* to deal with resistance to technologies like gender binaries, the relationship of sex and gender, parenthood, and family structure, all of which were formerly taken for granted in the common conceptions of such phenomena.

Heidegger was right; this is a dangerous process. As these questions and issues receive attention, they are not under anybody's control. In questioning one kind of transgression, Dasein may come to accept it as being familiar, producing a discourse that renders it intelligible. As more transgender individuals come out of the closet, types of gender transgression will no doubt become more intelligible to *das Man*, through the reiteration of this practice and its visibility. But this acceptance in familiarity opens the path for further transgression to be revealed, and to be rendered intelligible in turn, as others individuate within a context that rendered the first transgression intelligible. The field of possibility will have changed, making further questioning possible. The questions that will arise in the future are not conceivable as of yet; the conditions of their being asked have yet to happen. Setting out on the path of questioning means not being in control of where the inquiry will end up. (This is why philosophers must be brave.) Questioning is not a tool, used with an end in mind, but rather the precondition for tools, among other phenomena, to be meaningful at all. What is known is that Dasein, as the being to whom Being matters, is always engaged in this process.

This process is not, of course, limited to me; nor is it limited to transgressive Dasein or even to gender. My experience is simply the example I use in this project to illustrate what all are always already engaged in doing to varying degrees. The issue of gender is important in the West at this time, deeply important, but the operations of power it renders visible and intelligible are always at work, always exercising themselves in new and meaningful ways, ways that in turn create meaningfulness anew and establish models of truth for Dasein's ownmost potentiality-for-Being. Power is not merely a thing that some have and others lack; it is the exercise of the tension between any given technology or conceptual framework (*Gestell*) and the resistance that both transgresses and defines it. Power must be exercised on bodies and also arises out of resistance. There is no power without resistance. Political and ethical discourses are concerned with particular technologies of power, but power itself is always present, always exercised in whatever discourse is available. Understanding the operations of power at work in any given situation is therefore crucial to political and ethical conclusions regarding power. When any transgressive group attains emancipation by means of political and ethical prescription, it does not put a halt to the operations of power deployed against itself. It exercises power differently but always in a way that constitutes resistance of one sort or another. So even when gender transgressors attain political equality and social acceptance, there will not be an end to abjection. A new form of resistance, one that varies the theme yet again, will arise. This prospect may appear bleak and pessimistic, but it also contains its own "saving power." There will be new cases of the abjection of transgressors, to be sure, but this abjection will again force authentic evaluation of existing norms and create new potentialities-for-Being in Dasein's understanding of itself and its world. It has never been any other way.

Notes

1. Heidegger, "The Question Concerning Technology," 339.
2. Ibid.
3. Michel Foucault, "Technologies of the Self," in *Ethics: Subjectivity and Truth*, ed. Paul Rabinow, trans. Robert Hurley (New York: New Press, 1994), 225.
4. Ibid.
5. Michel Foucault, *The History of Sexuality*, vol. 3, *Care of the Self*, trans. Robert Hurley (New York: Vintage Books, 1986), 45–68.
6. Merleau-Ponty, *Signs*, 67.
7. Husserl, *Ideas: Second Book*, 283.
8. Butler, *Gender Trouble*, 43–44.
9. See Ludwig Wittgenstein, *Philosophical Investigations*, trans. G. E. M. Anscombe (Malden, MA: Blackwell, 2001), pt. 1, sec. 66–89.
10. David M. Halperin, *How to Do the History of Homosexuality* (Chicago: University of Chicago Press, 2002), 32–38.
11. Merleau-Ponty, *Signs*, 310 (emphasis in original).
12. For a similar analysis to the one in this section, see Janssen, "Queering Heidegger."
13. Heidegger, "The Question Concerning Technology," 314.
14. Heidegger, *Being and Time*, 24; H. 5.
15. See Andrew Feenberg, *Questioning Technology* (New York: Routledge, 1999).
16. Heidegger, "The Question Concerning Technology," 333.
17. Ibid., 338.

Bibliography

The works in this list that are not explicitly cited in the chapters were consulted for general information and have informed the author's analysis.

Ahmed, Sara. *Queer Phenomenology: Orientations, Objects, Others.* Durham, NC: Duke University Press, 2006.

Aho, Kevin. "Gender and Time: Revisiting the Question of Dasein's Neutrality." *Epoché* 12, no. 1 (2007): 137–155.

American Psychiatric Association. *Diagnostic and Statistical Manual of Mental Disorders.* 5th ed. Arlington, VA: American Psychiatric Association, 2013.

American Psychological Association. "Answers to Your Questions about Individuals with Intersex Conditions." 2006. http://www.apa.org/topics/lgbt/intersex.aspx.

Aquinas, Thomas. *Summa Theologica.* Translated by Fathers of the English Dominican Province. New York: Benziger Bros., 1947.

Aristotle. *The Complete Works of Aristotle.* Edited and translated by Jonathan Barnes. Vol. 1, *Generation of Animals.* Princeton, NJ: Princeton University Press, 1984.

———. *Politics.* Edited and translated by Ernest Barker. New York: Oxford University Press, 1946.

Augustine. *Confessions.* Translated by Henry Chadwick. Oxford: Oxford University Press, 1991.

Bailey, J. M., and R. C. Pillard. "A Genetic Study of Male Sexual Orientation." *Archives of General Psychiatry* 48, no. 12 (1991): 1089–1095.

Beatie, Thomas. "Labor of Love." *The Advocate,* March 14, 2008. http://www.advocate.com/news/2008/03/14/labor-love.

Beauvoir, Simone de. *The Ethics of Ambiguity.* Translated by Bernard Frechtman. New York: Citadel Press, 1948.

———. *The Second Sex.* Edited and translated by H. M. Parshley. New York: Vintage Books, 1952.

Benjamin, Harry. *The Transsexual Phenomenon.* New York: Julian Press, 1966.

Brown, Robbie. "Transgender Candidate Who Ran as Woman Did Not Mislead Voters, Court Says." *New York Times*, October 6, 2008. http://www.nytimes.com/2008/10/07/us/07gender.html.

Buijs, Carl. "A New Perspective on an Old Topic" thread. *Soc.support.transgendered*, April 16, 1996. http://groups.google.com/group/soc.support.transgendered/msg/184850df15e48963?hl=en.

Butler, Judith. "Arguing with the Real." In *Bodies That Matter: On the Discursive Limits of "Sex,"* 187–222. New York: Routledge, 1993.

———. "Bodies That Matter," in *Bodies That Matter: On the Discursive Limits of "Sex,"* 27–56. New York: Routledge, 1993.

———. "Dangerous Crossings: Willa Cather's Masculine Names." In *Bodies That Matter: On the Discursive Limits of "Sex,"* 143–166. New York: Routledge, 1993.

———"Doing Justice to Someone: Sex Reassignment and Allegories of Transsexuality." In *Undoing Gender*, 57–74. New York: Routledge, 2004.

———. "Gender Regulations." In *Undoing Gender*, 40–56. New York: Routledge, 2004.

———. *Gender Trouble: Feminism and the Subversion of Identity*. New York: Routledge, 1990.

———. "Introduction." In *Bodies That Matter: On the Discursive Limits of "Sex,"* 1–26. New York: Routledge, 1993.

———. "Phantasmatic Identification and the Assumption of Sex." In *Bodies That Matter: On the Discursive Limits of "Sex,"* 93–120. New York: Routledge, 1993.

———. "Preface." In *Bodies That Matter: On the Discursive Limits of "Sex,"* ix–xii. New York: Routledge, 1993.

Bynum, Caroline Walker. "The Body of Christ in the Later Middle Ages: A Reply to Leo Steinberg." In *Fragmentation and Redemption: Essays on Gender and the Human Body in Medieval Religion*, 79–118. New York: Zone Books, 1991.

———. "'. . . And Woman His Humanity': Female Imagery in the Religious Writing of the Later Middle Ages." In *Fragmentation and Redemption: Essays on Gender and the Human Body in Medieval Religion*, 151–180. New York: Zone Books, 1991.

Califia, Pat. *Public Sex: The Culture of Radical Sex*. San Francisco: Cleis Press, 1994.

———. *Speaking Sex to Power: The Politics of Queer Sex*. San Francisco: Cleis Press, 2002.

Caputo, John D. "The Absence of Monica: Heidegger, Derrida, and Augustine's *Confessions*." In *Feminist Interpretations of Martin Heidegger*, edited by Nancy J. Holland and Patricia Huntington, 149–164. University Park: Pennsylvania State University Press, 2001.

———. *Demythologizing Heidegger*. Indianapolis: Indiana University Press, 1993.

Chanter, Tina. "The Problematic Normative Assumptions of Heidegger's Ontology." In *Feminist Interpretations of Martin Heidegger*, edited by Nancy J. Holland and Patricia Huntington, 73–108. University Park: Pennsylvania State University Press, 2001.

Chase, Cheryl. "Hermaphrodites with Attitude: Mapping the Emergence of Intersex Political Activism." In *The Transgender Studies Reader*, edited by Susan Stryker and Stephen Whittle, 300–314. New York: Routledge, 2006.

Clement of Alexandria. "Paedagogus." In *The Ante-Nicene Fathers: Translations of the Writings of the Fathers Down to A.D. 325*, edited by Alexander Roberts and James Donaldson, 207–297. Peabody, MA: Hendrickson, 1994.

Derrida, Jacques. "Geschlecht: Sexual Difference, Ontological Difference." In *Feminist Interpretations of Martin Heidegger*, edited by Nancy J. Holland and Patricia Huntington, 53–72. University Park: Pennsylvania State University Press, 2001.

Descartes, René. *Meditations on First Philosophy*. Translated by Donald A. Cress. Indianapolis, IN: Hackett, 1993.

Dover, K. J. *Greek Homosexuality*. Cambridge, MA: Harvard University Press, 1978.

Dreyfus, Hubert. *Being-in-the-World: A Commentary on Heidegger's Being and Time, Division I*. Cambridge, MA: MIT Press, 1990.

Eco, Umberto. "Ur-Fascism." *New York Review of Books*, June 22, 1995. http://www.nybooks.com/articles/1995/06/22/ur-fascism.

Einiger, Josh. "Man Indicted in Shinnecock Baby Death." *ABC News*, August 11, 2010. http://abclocal.go.com/wabc/story?section=news/local&id=7605381.

Eugenides, Jeffrey. *Middlesex*. New York: Farrar, Straus and Giroux, 2002.

Euripides. *The Bacchae*. Translated by David Grene and Richmond Lattimore. Chicago: University of Chicago Press, 1959.

Fantz, Ashley. "An Ohio Transgender Teen's Suicide, a Mother's Anguish." *CNN*, January 4, 2015. http://www.cnn.com/2014/12/31/us/ohio-transgender-teen-suicide/.

Fausto-Sterling, Anne. *Sexing the Body: Gender Politics and the Construction of Sexuality*. New York: Basic Books, 2000.

Feenberg, Andrew. *Questioning Technology*. New York: Routledge, 1999.

Foucault, Michel. *The History of Sexuality*. Vol. 1, *An Introduction*. Translated by Robert Hurley. New York: Vintage Books, 1978.

———. *The History of Sexuality*. Vol. 2, *The Use of Pleasure*. Translated by Robert Hurley. New York: Vintage Books, 1985.

———. *The History of Sexuality*. Vol. 3, *The Care of the Self*, translated by Robert Hurley. New York: Vintage Books, 1986.

———. "Introduction." In *Herculine Barbin: Being the Recently Discovered Memoirs of a Nineteenth-Century French Hermaphrodite*, vii–xvii. Translated by Richard McDougall. New York: Pantheon Books, 1980.

———. *The Order of Things: An Archaeology of the Human Sciences*. New York: Random House, 1970.

———. "A Preface to Transgression." In *Aesthetics, Method, and Epistemology*, edited by James D. Faubion, translated by Donald F. Bouchard and Sherry Simon, 69–88. New York: New Press, 1994.

———. "Technologies of the Self." In *Ethics: Subjectivity and Truth*, edited by Paul Rabinow, translated by Robert Hurley, 223–252. New York: New Press, 1994.

Freud, Sigmund. "The Sexual Aberrations." In *Three Essays on the Theory of Sexuality*, edited and translated by James Strachey, 1–38. New York: Basic Books, 2000.

Garcia, Michelle. "School District Mum on Trans Teacher." *The Advocate*, October 17, 2008. http://www.advocate.com/news/2008/10/17/school-district-mum-trans-teacher.

Goldberg, Alan B., and Katie N. Thomson. "Barbara Walters Exclusive: Pregnant Man Expecting Second Child." *ABC News*, November 13, 2008. http://abcnews.go.com/Health/Story?id=6244878.

Green, Jamison. *Becoming a Visible Man*. Nashville, TN: Vanderbilt University Press, 2004.

Halberstam, Judith. *Female Masculinity*. Durham, NC: Duke University Press, 1998.

———. "Transgender Butch: Butch/FTM Border Wars and the Masculine Continuum." *GLQ: A Journal of Lesbian and Gay Studies* 4, no. 2 (1998): 287–310.

Hale, Jacob. "Are Lesbians Women?" In *The Transgender Studies Reader*, edited by Susan Stryker and Stephen Whittle, 281–299. New York: Routledge, 2006.

Halperin, David. *How to Do the History of Homosexuality*. Chicago: University of Chicago Press, 2002.

———. *One Hundred Years of Homosexuality and Other Essays on Greek Love*. New York: Routledge, 1990.

Halsall, Paul. "The Questioning of John Rykener, a Male Cross-Dressing Prostitute, 1395." Fordham University, May 1998. http://www.fordham.edu/halsall/source/1395rykener.html.

Hartness, Erin. "Cult-like Group Behaviors Come out in Court." *WRAL*, October 18, 2011. http://www.wral.com/news/local/story/9836148/.

Haugeland, John. "Heidegger on Being a Person." In *Dasein Disclosed: John Haugeland's Heidegger*, 3–16. Cambridge, MA: Harvard University Press, 2013.

Heidegger, Martin. *Being and Time*. Translated by John Macquarrie and Edward Robinson. San Francisco: HarperCollins, 1962.

———. "Memorial Address." In *Discourse on Thinking*, translated by John M. Anderson and E. Hans Freund, 43–57. New York: Harper and Row, 1966.

———. *The Metaphysical Foundations of Logic*. Translated by Michael Heim. Indianapolis: Indiana University Press, 1984.

———. "Only a God Can Save Us: *Der Spiegel*'s Interview with Martin Heidegger." *Philosophy Today* 20, No. 4 (1976): 267–284.

———. "The Origin of the Work of Art." In *Martin Heidegger: Basic Writings*, edited by David Farrell Krell, translated by Albert Hofstadter, 139–212. San Francisco: HarperCollins, 1993.

———. "The Question Concerning Technology." In *Basic Writings*, edited by David Farrell Krell, translated by William Lovitt, 307–342. San Francisco: HarperCollins, 1993.

———. *Sein und Zeit*. Tübingen, Germany: Max Niemeyer Verlag, 2001.

———. "The Turning." In *The Question Concerning Technology*, translated by William Lovitt, 36–52. New York: Harper and Row, 1977.

———. "What Is Metaphysics?" In *Martin Heidegger: Basic Writings*, edited by David Farrell Krell, translated by Albert Hofstadter, 89–110. San Francisco: HarperCollins, 1993.

Heinämaa, Sara. *Toward a Phenomenology of Sexual Difference: Husserl, Merleau-Ponty, Beauvoir*. New York: Rowman and Littlefield, 2003.

Herodotus. *The History*. Translated by David Grene. Chicago: University of Chicago Press, 1987.

Hirschfeld, Magnus. *Men and Women: The World Journey of a Sexologist*. Translated by Oliver P. Green. New York: G. P. Putnam's Sons, 1935.

———. *Transvestites: The Erotic Drive to Cross-Dress*. Translated by Michael A. Lombardi-Nash. Buffalo, NY: Prometheus Books, 1991.

Hole, John W., Jr. *Human Anatomy and Physiology*. Dubuque, IA: Wm. C. Brown, 1978.

Holland, Nancy J. "'The Universe Is Made of Stories, Not of Atoms': Heidegger and the Feminine They-Self." In *Feminist Interpretations of Martin Heidegger*, edited by

Nancy J. Holland and Patricia Huntington, 128–148. University Park: Pennsylvania State University Press, 2001.

Hotchkiss, Valerie R. Appendix to *Clothes Make the Man: Female Cross Dressing in Medieval Europe*, 131–142. New York: Garland, 1996.

Hrdy, Sarah Blaffer. *Mother Nature: A History of Mothers, Infants, and Natural Selection*. New York: Vintage, 2000.

Husserl, Edmund. *Ideas Pertaining to a Pure Phenomenology and to a Phenomenological Philosophy: First Book, General Introduction to a Pure Phenomenology*. Translated by F. Kersten. Boston: Kluwer Academic, 1983.

———. *Ideas Pertaining to a Pure Phenomenology and to a Phenomenological Philosophy: Second Book, Studies in the Phenomenology of Constitution*. Translated by Richard Rojcewicz and André Schuwer. Boston: Kluwer Academic, 1989.

Intersex Society of North America. "How Common Is Intersex?" http://www.isna.org/faq/frequency (accessed January 20, 2017).

———. "Our Mission." http://www.isna.org/ (accessed January 20, 2017).

Irigaray, Luce. "This Sex Which Is Not One." In *This Sex Which Is Not One*, translated by Catherine Porter and Carolyn Burke, 23–33. Ithaca, NY: Cornell University Press, 1985.

Janssen, E. Das. "Queering Heidegger: An Applied Ontology." *Radical Philosophy Review* 16, no. 3 (2013): 747–762.

———. "Technologies of Gender: Heidegger, Foucault, and the Saving Power." Paper presented at the Fifty-Second Meeting of the Society for Phenomenology and Existential Philosophy, Eugene, OR, October 24–26, 2013.

Jerome. "Commentarius in Epistolam ad Ephesios." In *Patrologica Latina*, edited by J. P. Minge, vol. 26. Paris: Garnier, 1884.

Kant, Immanuel. "An Answer to the Question, What Is Enlightenment?" In *Perpetual Peace and Other Essays on Politics, History, and Morals*, translated by Ted Humphrey, 41–48. Indianapolis, IN: Hackett, 1983.

Laqueur, Thomas. *Making Sex: Body and Gender from the Greeks to Freud*. Cambridge, MA: Harvard University Press, 1990.

Leland, Dorothy. "Conflictual Culture and Authenticity: Deepening Heidegger's Account of the Social." In *Feminist Interpretations of Martin Heidegger*, edited by Nancy J. Holland and Patricia Huntington, 109–127. University Park: Pennsylvania State University Press, 2001.

Lelchuck, Ilene. "When Is It OK for Boys to Be Girls, and Girls to Be Boys?" *San Francisco Chronicle*, August 27, 2006. http://www.sfgate.com/cgi-bin/article.cgi?file=/c/a/2006/08/27/MNGL2KQ8H41.DTL.

LeVay, Simon. "A Difference in Hypothalamic Structure between Heterosexual and Homosexual Men." *Science* 253 (1991): 1034–1037.

Lorde, Audre. *Sister Outsider: Essays and Speeches*. Trumansburg, NY: Crossing Press, 1984.

McWhorter, Ladelle. *Bodies and Pleasures: Foucault and the Politics of Sexual Normalization*. Indianapolis: Indiana University Press, 1999.

Merleau-Ponty, Maurice. *Phenomenology of Perception*. Translated by Colin Smith. New York: Routledge, 1962.

———. *Signs*. Translated by Richard C. McCleary. Chicago: Northwestern University Press, 1964.

Mill, John Stuart. "The Subjection of Women." In *The Basic Writings of John Stuart Mill*, edited by Dale E. Miller, 123–232. New York: Modern Library, 2002.

Money, John. "Hermaphroditism, Gender and Precocity in Hyperadrenocorticism: Psychologic Findings." *Bulletin of the Johns Hopkins Hospital* 96, no. 6 (1955): 253–264.

Moore, John Rees. "Voyaging with Odysseus: The Wile and Resilience of Virtue." *Humanitas* 8, no. 1 (2000): 103–127.

Nietzsche, Friedrich. *Beyond Good and Evil*. Translated by Walter Kaufmann. New York: Vintage Books, 1966.

———. *On the Genealogy of Morals*. Translated by Carol Diethe. Cambridge: Cambridge University Press, 1994.

Noddings, Nel. *Caring: A Feminine Approach to Ethics and Moral Education*. Berkeley: University of California Press, 1984.

Plato. *Republic*. Translated by Paul Shorey. In *The Collected Dialogues of Plato*, edited by Edith Hamilton and Huntington Cairns, 575–844. Princeton, NJ: Princeton University Press, 1938.

———. *Symposium*. Translated by Michael Joyce. In *The Collected Dialogues of Plato*, edited by Edith Hamilton and Huntington Cairns, 526–574. Princeton, NJ: Princeton University Press, 1938.

Power, Kim. *Veiled Desire: Augustine on Women*. New York: Continuum, 1996.

"Pregnant US Man Hails 'Miracle.'" *BBC News*, April 4, 2008. http://news.bbc.co.uk/2/hi/americas/7330196.stm.

Prosser, Jay. *Second Skins: The Body Narratives of Transsexuality*. New York: Columbia University Press, 1998.

Raymond, Janice G. *The Transsexual Empire: The Making of the She-Male*. New York: Teachers College Press, 1994.

Rice University. "Is 'the Dress' White and Gold or Blue and Black? Visual Perception Expert Weighs In." *Science Daily*, March 2, 2015. http://www.sciencedaily.com/releases/2015/03/150302134235.htm.

Rodemeyer, Lanei. "Transsexuality, Phenomenology, and Discourse." Paper presented at the Society for Phenomenology and Existential Philosophy, Philadelphia, PA, October 2006.

Rogers, Thomas. "What the Pregnant Man Didn't Deliver." *Salon*, July 3, 2008. http://www.salon.com/mwt/feature/2008/07/03/pregnant_man/index.html?source=newsletter.

Rosin, Hanna. "A Boy's Life." *The Atlantic*, November 2008. http://theatlantic.com/doc/200811/transgender-children.

Rubin, Gayle. *Deviations: A Gayle Rubin Reader*. Durham, NC: Duke University Press, 2011.

Rubin, Henry S. "Phenomenology as Method in Trans Studies." *GLQ: A Journal of Lesbian and Gay Studies* 4, no. 2 (1998): 263–282.

Russell, Bertrand. *The Problems of Philosophy*. Indianapolis, IN: Hackett, 1912.

Saillant, Catherine. "School Blamed in Killing of Gay Student." *Los Angeles Times*, May 8, 2008. http://www.latimes.com/news/printedition/california/la-me-oxnard8-2008may08,0,6901056.story.

———. "Teen in Gay-Student Slaying Case Agrees to 21-Year Prison Term." *Los Angeles Times*, November 21, 2011. http://latimesblogs.latimes.com/lanow/2011/11/gay-slaying.html.

Sawicki, Jana. "Heidegger and Foucault: Escaping Technological Nihilism." In *Foucault and Heidegger: Critical Encounters*, edited by Alan Milchman and Alan Rosenberg, 55–73. Minneapolis: University of Minnesota Press, 2003.

———. "Identity Politics and Sexual Freedom." In *Disciplining Foucault: Feminism, Power, and the Body*, 33–48. New York: Routledge, 1991.

Sheets-Johnstone, Maxine. *The Roots of Power: Animate Form and Gendered Bodies*. Chicago: Open Court, 1994.

Simons, Margaret A. *Beauvoir and the Second Sex: Feminism, Race, and the Origins of Existentialism*. New York: Rowman and Littlefield, 1999.

Spinosa, Charles, Fernando Flores, and Hubert L. Dreyfus. *Disclosing New Worlds: Entrepreneurship, Democratic Action, and the Cultivation of Solidarity*. Cambridge, MA: MIT Press, 1997.

Spivak, Gayatri Chakravorty. "In a Word: Interview." Interview by Ellen Rooney. In *The Essential Difference*, edited by Naomi Schor and Elizabeth Weed, 151–184. Indianapolis: Indiana University Press, 1994.

Stryker, Susan. "(De)Subjugated Knowledges: An Introduction to Transgender Studies." In *The Transgender Studies Reader*, edited by Susan Stryker and Stephen Whittle, 1–18. New York: Routledge, 2006.

———. *Transgender History*. Berkeley, CA: Seal Studies, 2008.

Stryker, Susan, and Stephen Whittle, eds. *The Transgender Studies Reader*. New York: Routledge, 2006.

Swaffar, Gar. "Pregnant Man Separates from Wife." *Digital Journal*, April 20, 2012. http://www.digitaljournal.com/article/323324.

Tolstoy, Leo. *The Death of Ivan Ilych*. Translated by Aylmer Maude and J. D. Duff. New York: Penguin Group, 2003.

Vitello, Paul. "The Trouble When Jane Becomes Jack." *New York Times*, August 20, 2006. http://query.nytimes.com/gst/fullpage.html?res=9802EEDD153EF933A1575B C0A9609C8B63.

Whittle, Stephen. "Where Did We Go Wrong? Feminism and Trans Theory—Two Teams on the Same Side." In *The Transgender Studies Reader*, edited by Susan Stryker and Stephen Whittle, 194–204. New York: Routledge, 2006.

Wilchins, Riki. *Queer Theory, Gender Theory: An Instant Primer*. Los Angeles: Alyson Books, 2004.

Wittgenstein, Ludwig. *Philosophical Investigations*. Translated by G. E. M. Anscombe. Malden, MA: Blackwell, 2001.

Wollstonecraft, Mary. *A Vindication of the Rights of Women*. Edited by Carol H. Poston. New York: W. W. Norton, 1987.

Index

logical method and, 19; questioning its existence, 4; and self, 103; structures of, 20; transgressive, 90, 135; understanding it will die, 22–24; uniqueness of each, 25, 27; and variations on theme of gender normativity, 113. *See also* fallen Dasein; *Mitsein* ("Being-with")

das Man: Dasein and, 24; and discourses of power, 87–88; divisions within, 27, 32, 117; as enframing Dasein, 122; exclusion from, 117; gender constructed by, 84; and insistence on binary system, 101; and leg shaving, 104–105; as maintaining "how things are done," 109–110; and male and female ways of sitting, 109; normativization by, 102; pioneers of change within, 110; presuppositions of, 26; as social body, 2; as the "they," 21; and the uncanny, 109; variations on a theme within, 113; and will to conformity, 102

death, facing, 22–24, 27, 29
The Death of Ivan Ilych (Tolstoy), 24
dees and toms, 39n18
"de-realizing" the present, 48
Derrida, Jacques, 72
Descartes, René, 19–20, 67
Dionysus, 52
disclosive phenomena, gender as, 24
"Discourse on Thinking" (Heidegger), 99
discourse(s): breakdown of, 87; defined, 96n55, 104; of knowledge and power, 81, 104
"disorders of sex development," 2
doer and deed, 110
dominant factions, 91–92
drag performers: as transgressive, 10; versus transvestic fetishism, 7; use of parody by, 110
dualistic models: mind-body relationship, 47, 99; transgression defining within, 101, 106; two-sex model, 49, 56–57, 63

Eco, Umberto, 96n60
embodiment: Foucault on, 79–87; Husserl on, 74–77, 84–85; Merleau-Ponty on, 77–79, 85; as theme in Heidegger's work, 32, 67

empathy, 98–99
Employment Non-Discrimination Act, 5
enframing (*Gestell*), 99–100, 116–117, 126–128, 133–136
Enlightenment era, 56–57, 63
Equal Rights Act, 5
equal treatment political demands, 61
equipment: entities as, 20–21; relations as, 27
essentialism: biological, 13–14, 26, 43, 102, 108; "the feminine" in, 97–98; gender theories of, 13, 26, 97–98
Eugenides, Jeffrey, 1–2
everyday, philosophy of the, 73
excess in religion and sexuality, 82
existence that experiences, 19
existential origins of gender, 3
experiencer, Dasein as, 18, 30
extramarital sex, 16

fallen Dasein: and authenticity, 23, 28–29; and common sense, 109–110; and *das Man*, 28, 88; in default state of Being, 88; and discourses of power, 87–88; and Foucault, 86, 87; gender and, 103; Heidegger's definition of, 21, 103–104; and individuation, 115; as the they-self, 21, 23; and uncanniness, 28–29, 114
"family resemblances" between things, 131
fanaticism, 101–102
"fanciful idealization," 110
fatherhood: Christian restrictions regarding, 53; in Greek social system, 50; legal definition of, 12
fear and Dasein, 27–28
femininity: in ancient Greece, 49–53; and building a coherent identity, 108; in Christian era, 53–54; and empathy, 99; in essentialist theory, 97–98; females as imperfect males, 49–50; as a flaw, 97–98; within masculine parameters, 13; as Other, 14–15, 98, 108; and rationality, 14, 99; as unifying element, 14. *See also* women
feminism: and biological essentialism, 13–14, 97–98; building a theory of, 108; in Enlightenment era, 57; and Heidegger, 32; and inclusion of transgender persons, 107; and transsexualism, 95–96n45

EPHRAIM DAS JANSSEN does research in the areas of phenomenology and queer studies, with particular emphasis on lived experience and practical application of philosophical theory in the furtherance of social justice.

CPSIA information can be obtained
at www.ICGtesting.com
Printed in the USA
LVHW11s2056161018
593810LV00004B/363/P